SHOPPING CENTER SECURITY

Perception and Reality

Donald H. Greene

International Council of Shopping Centers

About the International Council of Shopping Centers

The International Council of Shopping Centers (ICSC) is the trade association of the shopping center industry. Serving the shoppinc center industry since 1957, ICSC is a non-for-profit organization with more than 53,000 members in 98 countries worldwide.

ICSC members include shopping center

- owners
- developers
- managers
- marketing specialists
- leasing agents
- retailers
- researchers
- attorneys

- architects
- contractors
- consultants
- investors
- lenders and brokers
- academics
- public officials

ICSC sponsors approximtely 200 meetings a year and provides a wide array of services and products for shopping center professionals, including publications and research data.

For more information about ICSC, please contact:
International Council of Shopping Centers
1221 Avenue of the Americas
New York, NY 10020-1099
Telephone (646) 728-3800
Fax: (212) 589-5555
www.icsc.org

Companies, professional groups, clubs and other organizations may qualify for special terms when ordering quantities of more than 20 of this title.

Published by
International Council of Shopping Centers
Publications Department
1221 Avenue of the Americas
New York, NY 10020-1099
www.icsc.org

Cover photographs courtesy of The Macerich Company

International Standard Book Number 1-58268-049-3

ICSC Catalog Number: 236

To my wife, Margie, who endured many months of my emotional ups and downs as I worked at putting this manuscript together, hopefully in an interesting and informative way. Your tolerance, thoughts, ideas, criticism and correction truly helped me along the way.

I know proofreading my work is a REAL chore!!

Thank you!

Contents

Preface

Shopping Center Security—Perception and Reality was written in recognition of the ever-increasing demand and need for security at public-access properties. We have organized the book with the foundational material in the early chapters followed by chapters that contain a number of suggestion and recommendation lists from which developers, owners, managers, or security directors may make informed selections based on factors that may influence security requirements at their center. While we have attempted to present a comprehensive guide to many areas of shopping center security, this book should not be relied upon as a single source of reference. Some of the recommendations and/or suggestions for security procedures, measures and controls discussed in this text may not be applicable to your center.

The security procedures, measures and controls discussed and listed in this book should not be considered as shopping center industry standards or best practices. Clearly, a property's location, configuration, tenant mix, demographics, use(s), crime history and other factors must be considered in reaching an informed decision concerning the components of the security plan.

It is our hope that the material presented in this text is useful to all readers in developing and/or evaluating your security function.

Acknowledgments

It is my sincere hope that everyone who reads this text takes away one concept, idea or suggestion that helps to make their property a safer place for patrons, employees, tenants, vendors and visitors. Much of the content of this book has come from my association with many knowledgable and experienced security professionals. I have attempted to impart much of the wisdom I gained from them in *Shopping Center Security—Perception and Reality* so that you, the readers, are the benefactors of their collective expertise. I am truly thankful for our professional relationship.

Recognizing that some incidents that occur at shopping centers may result in allegations of inadequate security, I asked a number of skilled premises security attorneys to review portions of this book from a legal perspective. Here, I formally acknowledge and thank those lawyers who were kind enough to review and comment on this text.

Kenneth M. Alweis, Esq.
Fix Spindelman Brovitz & Goldman
Syracuse, NY

Arik Arad, President & CEO
ArCon Security Corp.
New York, NY

Robert Harrington, Security Director
Pyramid Management Company
Syracuse, NY

Howard Kaplan, President & CEO
IPC International Corporation
Bannockburn, Illinois

John Lusher, Senior VP
IPC International Corporation
Bannockburn, Illinois

Nicole Mauskopf, Esq.
Wilson Elser Moskowitz Edelman &
    Dicker
New York, NY

ACKNOWLEDGMENTS

Jack Miller, Esq.
Regnier, Taylor, Curran & Eddy
Hartford, CT

Barry Rothman, Esq.
Strongin Rothman & Abrams
New York, NY

There are many more people to whom I am extremely thankful but who I have not included in this list. Please know that I am deeply appreciative.

To the International Council of Shopping Centers, thank you for the opportunity to author such an important book in these difficult times. I am very grateful for the confidence you placed in me.

The International Council of Shopping Centers would also like to acknowledge the following individuals who contributed their time and expertise in the review of this publication:

Elizabeth H. Belkin
Piper Rudnick
Chicago, IL

Scott Born
Valor Security
Marietta, GA

John Gerdes, SCSM, CLS, CPM
L&B Realty Advisors
Dallas, TX

David Levenberg
General Growth Properties, Inc.
Chicago, IL

Scott Petrie
Pennsylvania Real Estate Investment
   Trust
Philadelphia, PA

Tony Tomasella, SCSM
Advanced Tech Security Services, Inc.
Valencia, CA

Tom Walton
Allied Security
Norcross, GA

About the Author

Donald H. Greene served as a captain in the U.S. Marine Corps, was a special agent for the Federal Bureau of Investigation for nearly 30 years, and currently serves on the Criminal Justice Advisory Board at his alma mater, the State University of New York at Brockport.

In 1994 Mr. Greene accepted a position as Corporate Safety and Security Director for a large property developer and manager with a large portfolio of shopping centers. In 1996 he established Strategic Security Concepts, Inc., Skaneateles, New York, an independent security management firm that provides security management consulting services to public access facilities, including shopping centers. In addition, Mr. Greene is a forensic consultant, providing expert testimony in premises security matters and he is a guest lecturer on the subject of security management.

It is the author's hope that readers of this book become motivated by some of the suggestions in the text so that they take the "First Step" and closely examine each of their individual properties for risks and vulnerability. Where weaknesses are identified you may find a security measure, control or procedure cited in this book that may be helpful to your situation. Comments or questions concerning any of the material contained in this book may be directed to the author as follows:

telephone: 315-685-3978

e-mail: Dgreene@adelphia.net

website: www.securitystrategies.com

mailing address: Don Greene, President
Strategic Security Concepts, Inc.
P.O. Box 793
Skaneateles, NY 13152

Shopping Center Security—Perception and Reality was written to offer security suggestions and recommendations to shopping center developers, owners, and managers. The opinions, suggestions, views and recommendations contained in the text of this book are not to be considered *absolute* security guidelines, standards, or best practices for the shopping center industry, but instead only offer educational information.

Since all retail centers differ in size, building configuration, tenant composition, trade area, customer demographic, and many other influencing factors, appropriate and reasonable security practices, procedures, policies and measures for each property may also differ. ICSC does not recommend standards because it is not possible to develop security standards applicable to all shopping centers and it would be misleading to suggest that following the views contained in this book would satisfy a shopping center's security requirement and result in a safe property.

This book is intended to provide a broad spectrum of security management and operation options, some of which may have an application to your property. Every effort has been made to make this book as complete and accurate as possible; however, there are many other useful references available. A bibliography of some of those references is included at the end of this publication.

Neither the author nor publisher shall be liable to any person or entity for any loss or damage caused or alleged to be caused as a result of applying security techniques, practices, procedures, controls or measures discussed in this book.

Introduction

So many aspects of our lives and culture have changed in recent years that it's often difficult to keep up with the times. Medical science has conquered a number of illnesses that formerly claimed many lives far too early. Our life expectancy has been extended because of new and improved fitness and nutritional information and heightened awareness. Information technology, including the internet, communication satellites, and other forms of wireless transmission, has brought countries and continents ever closer.

The shopping centers that replaced our main streets of days gone by have evolved into destination locations complete with traditional retail, food courts and restaurants, theaters, entertainment components, recreational facilities and much more. Many shopping centers are connected to or associated with hotels. Developers and owners continue to create centers that appeal to and satisfy the needs and desires of everyone in the family. The more hours you spend at these new diverse centers, the more disposable income you are likely to spend.

While these new family entertainment and shopping venues often have many of the same components, they differ in many ways from the "shopping center" of old. Some centers are constructed around large open parking lots with individual tenant spaces facing the common lot; these properties are commonly referred to as "strip centers" or plazas. Other centers are contained within a single structure with a climate-controlled environment referred to as the common area or public space. Shopping centers may be spread out on one level with multiple wings or they may have multiple levels. Many centers are surrounded by sprawling parking areas while others may have attached multilevel parking garages or underground parking. Some centers stand alone between communities and serve as regional centers while others occupy city blocks and are surrounded by high-rise office space.

In short, shopping centers are dissimilar as much as they are similar. Much like the changes in medical science and information technology, the profile of shopping centers is ever-changing. With these evolving changes, so must security planning, management and operations change.

It is with this in mind that we have recognized the need to provide a guide to shopping center security. Because of the many differences in location, structure, tenant makeup and market demographics, and much more, there is no "one size fits all" as it relates to security at a shopping center. A security plan for a shopping center may differ as drastically as the very centers themselves. Much as our society and culture have changed with modern-day technology, so must security at shopping centers change with the new and ever-changing profile of these properties. Clearly, as the shopping center entices more patrons to remain longer at their property with many more diverse attractions, more consideration must be given to safety and security. We know that today's society is much more security-conscious and demands higher levels of security in virtually all environs.

In this book we intend to provide new public safety and security issues for shopping center owners, developers and managers to consider as they modernize existing centers or design and develop new properties. We will list and explain the steps that may be used in building a solid foundation for a security plan and we will provide management techniques for the components.

Recognizing that safety and security at a large public access facility such as a shopping center impacts patrons, tenants, vendors, employees and visitors, we will explain how each category of person can help individually and collectively in the overall security of the shopping center. Personal security practices for shoppers and employees and security expectations are included in the following pages.

It is truly our hope and desire that the contents of this book favorably impact safety and security at one of *the* most frequently visited public-access environments in our society—today's shopping, entertainment and dining centers.

1 | Perception and Reality

Perhaps the old adage "perception is reality" is an appropriate thought to keep in mind when discussing, planning and evaluating security at a shopping center. This simple statement reminds us that perception is what one becomes aware of through the use of senses or through a knowledge of his or her surroundings. Perception is an individual feeling or sense that is physically observed or mentally envisioned by an individual as a result of objects or events in his or her surroundings. Perception is truly individual or singular in nature. Two people in the same location at the same time may have a different perception of their environment, but in either case perception is reality to that person at that time.

Using "perception is reality" as a guidepost, and understanding the singular nature of *perception*, we can begin to formulate ideas, concepts and measures that together may create the perception of safety and security for customers, vendors, tenants and employees while at the same time creating a feeling of discomfort to would-be perpetrators. Clearly a positive *perception* can, and should, be created through the use and implementation of *real*, and effective, security measures, controls and practices.

Keeping in mind the individuality of your property and the singular nature of *perception* will aid in creating a site-specific conceptual safety and security plan that satisfies *your* needs and the desires of your patrons, employees and tenants.

Your security plan should provide for customer and employee safety while at the same time projecting a customer-friendly and helpful attitude. A proactive and positive security presence translates into favorable public relations. If patrons *perceive* a safe and secure environment, they are likely to spend greater amounts of time at your center and return frequently. It is highly likely that they will spread the word to friends, neighbors, and relatives that your center is safe, secure, and customer-friendly. Creating a warm, friendly and *safe* environment for customers—

perception - at your center clearly is conducive to good business while satisfying customer security concerns. To the customer, *perception is reality*.

It is universally recognized and acknowledged that employees are happier, more effective and more efficient when working in a desirable environment. An integral part of a pleasant workplace is safety and security for employees. In the instance of a shopping center, the term "employees" includes mall staff as well as tenant employees. If employees *perceive* a safe and secure environment based on what they see and hear each day as they work in the center, they are likely to feel appreciated and will meet and greet customers and visitors with a caring attitude. Since mall staff and tenant employees are recognized by patrons as symbols of the center, this positive attitude becomes another plus in your public relations efforts. By creating a *perceived* safe and secure work environment for employees, management derives another business advantage. To the employees, *perception is reality*.

The shopping center and all of its structural components are valued assets of the owners and managers. As such they require some level of protection. Your conceptual security plan should consider adequate protection of the property. Some of the standard and locally required measures such as fire alarms become visible signs of safety and security that are noticed by customers, enhancing their *perception* of a safe and secure environment. Directional, informational, or caution signage also sends messages of care and concern about organization and structure to patrons and employees. The assets protection component of your security plan aids in the *perception is reality* feeling.

To the would-be perpetrator, any and all evidence of security at a property means he is at higher risk to perform a criminal act. While no one is foolish enough to believe that security or police presence will eliminate all crime or criminal acts, it is widely understood that security measures are likely to deter many perpetrators. If a would-be perpetrator *perceives* that the security presence [physical or technical] at a property will detect his actions or identify him, he is likely to go to another location to effect his plan. To the perpetrator—*perception is reality*.

Keeping in mind that *perception is reality* to customers, employees and potential problem mall visitors, we can see how and why it is wise to give safety and security careful consideration as we develop new plans or as we evaluate existing safety and security operations and measures. Taking the concept of *perception* one step further, we can use the proactive safety and security measures we have planned or implemented to influence all of those who *perceive* positively to adopt the attitude that total safety and security is everyone's responsibility. This final step can only be taken after patrons, employees, vendors and visitors have individually generated a positive *perception* through real measures. If the property is *perceived* as safe and secure by everyone, it is likely that everyone will individually and collectively promote that *perception* to others because of their appreciation of the comfortable shopping and work environment. Security awareness will have been created and it will grow. To the entire shopping center—*perception is reality.*

As you read and analyze the many safety and security concepts discussed in this book, keep in mind *perception is reality* to everyone who comes on to your property.

Real visible measures and controls such as perimeter fencing, directional and informational signage, adequate parking lot lighting and recognizable security officers are a few of the security *realities* that go toward creating a positive *perception* at a property. *Real* measures produce a *real* positive *perception.* Perception is reality.

To be sure, nowhere in this text do we advocate or promote the creation of a false sense of security—a false perception. This book provides suggestions and recommendations for the development of *real* site-specific security measures, controls, practices and procedures that are likely to create a positive *perception*, because they *are real.* Clearly it would be foolhardy and irresponsible to purposely engage in security deception in an effort to create a positive *perception* of safety and security at a property.

2 | The Importance of Security

The safety and security function at an enclosed mall, strip center/plaza or community center has a number of important tasks. Many tasks may be accomplished or supported through the use of hardware, software, security officers or combinations of one or more of these resources. A number of roles are commonly and appropriately taken on by a security officer or a group of officers. Along with its primary function of assisting in customer and employee safety, security functions as protector of the property, customer service and information provider, risk manager, and rules enforcer. Security officers at most properties are called upon to monitor fire alarms and maintain order in the parking facilities and at points of ingress and egress. Security officers are commonly responsible for locking down the property at the close of business and often patrol long after normal retail hours, especially where centers have late-night entertainment or restaurant operations. Security officers and their supervisors are commonly the only remaining representatives of the center when retail and entertainment business has closed for the evening. The basic functional importance of security is really explained by the nature, diversity and constancy of its duties. No single aspect of the security function can, or should be, identified as more important, or the most important. A well-trained and supervised officer will go about his duties giving attention to each of his roles as the situation dictates. The high visibility and recognizable presence of security officers at the property establishes them as the front line of public relations.

Perception Is Reality

SECURITY AS PUBLIC SAFETY

An effective and efficient physical security operation should be designed to be highly visible. An easily recognizable and highly visible security presence is likely to serve as a deterrent to criminal activity. Security's presence at the property sends a comforting message to customers, tenants, vendors and employees while creating uneasiness for would-be perpetrators. A physical security presence also conveys a message of order, structure and assistance to those who come onto the property.

Prior to 9/11, many in our society would have preferred that security not be visible. Today's society scrutinizes security operations at most public-access environments. The general public is looking for, and expecting, visible signs of security everywhere they go. In fact, it is the visibility of security that makes people feel safe and secure. If the shopping public sees and *perceives* an effective and efficient physical security presence at your center, it is likely to spread the word to friends and neighbors, and they will regularly return to visit your center to shop. The same holds true for tenants, employees and visitors to the property.

While all security experts should agree that even the most sophisticated security function cannot stop all crime or terrorist-type actions, a well-thought out, site-specific security plan can and will effectively deter many criminal factors.

SECURITY AS A PROPERTY PROTECTOR

Through a designed series of interior and exterior patrols security officers, armed with post orders, can observe, report and/or address threats to customer, tenant or mall property. Acting in the role of property protectors, security officers oftentimes deter or interrupt vandalism or larceny. Again, the mere presence of a uniformed officer on patrol is likely to deter the would-be vandal or thief from breaking and entering an automobile or tenant space. During the late evening hours, with far less customer, tenant, and vehicular traffic on the property, security staffing is likely to be reduced; however, property protection responsibilities continue as they focus more on protection of the structure and its contents. Fire watch and signs of breaking and entering the building become of paramount importance.

SECURITY AS RISK MANAGER

With large numbers of patrons, tenant employees, vendors and mall employees moving in and about the center each day, it is important to minimize the opportunity for an accident. While most properties have contracted or proprietary housekeepers, janitorial, and maintenance staff personnel, security officers, if trained properly, are likely to observe safety hazards and report them for repair. Because security officers are required to move about the common area, service corridors and exterior of the center, they have a broad visual exposure to the entire property and can minimize risk of accidents by reporting trip hazards, faulty escalators, malfunctioning elevators or parking area problems. Acting in this capacity, security officers are able to contribute to the overall safety and security of the center.

SECURITY AS A RULES ENFORCER

Much as our society is built on structure and social order, any public-access facility should have local rules to provide for the safety and convenience of its visitors. Some community centers or strip centers may determine that they require nothing more than directional and informational signage in the parking areas. Larger enclosed super-regional malls may post a behavior code defining prohibited acts. In either instance, in order to insure the rules of order are obeyed, for the benefit of all, it may be necessary to enlist a security officer or have a periodic patrol arrangement with the local policing agency to enforce rules of the property. Clearly it is important to patrons, tenants, employees and visitors to shop in an orderly environment.

SECURITY AS CUSTOMER SERVICE AND INFORMATION PROVIDER

There can be no argument that at those properties where a highly visible security officer(s) is present, he/she is recognized by all as a representative of the property. Officers should be trained as "greeters." A number of studies and surveys have established that customers, particularly women, feel safer if they have been recognized by an officer as they enter the property. An officer greeting patrons as they enter the mall sends a very positive and reassuring message. The visitor has been recognized in a customer friendly way and the *perception* of effective, efficient security has begun.

Because security officers are easily identified as part of the mall staff, they are frequently asked questions regarding tenant location, special events, exit locations, etc. Customers, tenants, vendors and visitors consistently depend on security officers for a broad range of customer service support.

SECURITY AS PUBLIC RELATIONS REPRESENTATIVES

Safety and security is not merely the presence of an officer. It is a function carried out by an officer or group of officers. Where officers carry out that function, operating in a variety of very diverse roles, they become the person or persons to whom customers, tenants, employees and vendors look as the true functioning representative of the property. Typically patrons and/or employees may look to security in time of need—a lost child, a misplaced package, assistance in locating a car. If they have a positive experience in their time of need, that contact will go a long way toward enhancing or improving your center's image in the community. It's not necessary that the security officer find the misplaced package or immediately locate the car; his/her professionalism, confidence and bearing will send a message that conveys the effectiveness and efficiency of the security function. Through his/her actions the "public relations security officer" will have created a positive *perception* for the center and its safety and security function.

SECURITY AS A COMPONENT OF A COMFORTABLE SHOPPING ENVIRONMENT

Shopping centers, power centers, plazas, and community centers are developed to appeal to retail customers from all walks of life. The tenant makeup of a given property is likely to dictate its target customer. No matter the customer profile or the design and makeup of the property, patrons want to feel warm and cozy, safe and comfortable at their chosen destination.

As owners and developers create and improve shopping and entertainment venues, new and improved customer conveniences are included or added. Traffic flow in and out of convenient parking facilities pleases customers. Shopping and entertainment structures are designed to be pleasing to the eye and appealing to shoppers as they move about the property. Tenant storefronts are attractive and interior décor is engaging. In many instances, music is introduced into the environment. All in all, owners, developers, and managers recognize and acknowledge that it is very important to introduce a number of features that may encourage patrons to visit their center, remain for longer periods of time and return again and again.

In recent years no single component of the shopping center environment has gotten more attention than the security component. Society has become more security-conscious and expects higher levels of visible security. Customers no longer suspect the property is troubled if/when they observe security measures and controls; they consider that property management understands society's safety and security concerns and has positively responded. The security component of a shopping and entertainment venue, though it may differ in appearance and function, has clearly become another of the elements that go to make up that cozy, comfortable shopping environment patrons desire.

Recognizing that there are differences in virtually every shopping center, this book addresses how you can properly review and analyze your property and determine the necessary components of a site-specific security plan tailored exclusively to your center.

Through this examination of the many aspects of the security function, you may have gained a greater appreciation and understanding of "The Importance of Security" and how it can become an asset to total shopping center operations. In the following chapters, we will discuss the many ways property owners or managers may effectively implement, manage and utilize security measures, controls and procedures as a business advantage and as public safety providers—*Reality*.

3 | Step One—The Study

In considering safety and security requirements of a shopping center, it is first necessary to conduct an analysis of your center, such questions are: How are we different from other similar properties? What do we have in common with all/most other shopping centers? What external factors may impact our security needs? What internal factors or distinctive operations do we need to consider? What are our greatest risks? Where are our vulnerabilities?

There are many questions that must be asked and answered in evaluating an existing safety and security function and in developing a new security operation. The study and resulting identification of factors that may influence the level and kind of security required at your property, apart from all others, is called a risk analysis and threat assessment. The extent and detail required for this analysis and assessment may vary depending on the size of the center, its projected market share, its structural configuration and many other factors. This evaluation, in the instance of an existing property, or study, associated with a new property, should form the basis for a conceptual security plan. It should be conducted by a knowledgeable in-house security professional or a reputable independent security consultant who has no affiliation with security products or services. As is the case in the conduct of our business or personal lives, our plans should be based on a reasonable level of study and research.

Although virtually every shopping center can be generically referred to as a retail location comprised of a number of tenants, virtually all centers differ in many ways. A risk analysis and threat assessment will give consideration to those differences and result in a site-specific plan that is adequate and reasonable for a given property. No matter how formal or informal the evaluation or study, it should give consideration to four (4) basic categories:

1. Location of the Property
2. Nature and Use of the Property
3. Demographics
4. History of Crime on the Property or in the Area

Location of the Property
Consideration should be given to the proximity of the property to major highways and thoroughfares. Is the property served by or near public transportation? Is the center associated with or attached to a hotel or convention center?

Many questions relating to your center and its specific location within a city or state will help in gaining an understanding of the kind of risk(s) you are likely to expect.

Nature and Use of the Property
The nature and use of the property can easily be defined as a shopping center for retail sales. The security evaluation or study should identify specific uses within the shopping center and determine how those uses [tenants] may impact the overall security function.

Does the center have movie theaters? How many? What are the hours of operation? Are there late-night restaurants serving alcohol? While none of these uses individually effect the security operation, together, they may deserve consideration when making security decisions.

Demographics
Criminologists and sociologists agree that the economic conditions, education level, and stability of a community, along with a number of other demographic factors, are generally given consideration when predicting the likelihood of the occurrence of crime in a community or neighborhood. Therefore, it is important to examine the demographics of the community in which you are located as well as the demographics of the market share of your center.

History of Crime at the Property and/or in the Area
It is important to understand the volume and nature of crime that has occurred on a property in the past in order to establish a reasonable and adequate security level that may deter and diminish that level in the future. Crime history can be obtained from the police and a number of other sources.

The following outline, while it may not be all-inclusive for all properties, should serve as a guide to those preparing or contracting with a consultant to conduct a security evaluation or develop a new conceptual security plan:

A. Risk Analysis/Threat Assessment

- Understanding property location, nature and use, demographics and crime history
- Examination and study of the proposed structure/existing business and each of its components, annexes and parking facilities
- Understanding all of the activities planned for the property (aquarium, hotel, retail, other entertainment)
- Identification and evaluation of property assets to be protected
- Review and analysis of volume and nature of crime occurring at the property and in the neighborhood (past and present)
- Interview local police agency(s)—additional crime threat review and analysis
- Interview management team to determine business philosophy
- Examine and review existing safety and security functions and procedures
- Identify potential threats based upon the above study
- Isolate areas of risk and establish controls

Specific Areas to Consider

B. Perimeter Security
lighting
Crime Prevention Through Environmental Design (CPTED)
exterior patrol/parking garage
traffic flow
signage
property barriers

C. Access Control
alarms
gates
locking devices
employee entrances
loading dock procedures
courier service procedures
nonbusiness-hour access
key management
emergency response access (including police, fire and medical services)

D. Interior Security
guard tour system
service corridors

property rules signage
rest rooms
CCTV

E. Security Guard Management
hiring practices
training
development of security operations manual
creation of post orders
daily logs and incident reports
computerized incident reporting and tracking
officer uniforms and equipment
command and control center
staffing and deployment (methodology)

F. Police, Fire, Emergency Rescue
liaison
property familiarity
knowledge of emergency procedures
communications
routine response procedures—reporting to the property

G. Life Safety Issues
plans—
    evacuation
    disaster & recovery
communication procedures
procedures currently in effect
property hazards
safety and directional signage

In addition to the above, shopping center management should expect that a good security evaluation and/or study should include the below listed considerations:

ADVANCED ANALYSIS OF EXISTING FACILITY AND/OR PLANNED EXPANSION

➢ review special activities and functions planned for the mall that may impact security
➢ identification and profile of the target shopper
➢ environmental and structural design issues effecting security

➤ consider developing security trends and experience factors at similar shopping center facilities

➤ identify special groups, organizations, or nearby facilities that may impact mall security

➤ develop the current and future level of police service provided by the police department

A typical finding as a result of this systematic study or evaluation may result in a listing of the types of reasonably foreseeable criminal activity that may be expected at a given property. A sample finding follows:

- larceny/petit theft—shoplifting—purse snatching
- robbery—(of) merchant, bank/ATM, mall patron, employee, parking facility patron
- credit card fraud
- auto theft—possible carjacking
- theft from auto—vehicle break-in
- possession of firearm or dangerous weapon
- assault—in conjunction with robbery (or attempt)—fight
- domestic disputes—customer–merchant disputes
- disruptive youth—potentially youth gangs
- insurance fraud—slip and fall—escalator accidents—auto theft

The conclusions reached after a reasonable scientific and systematic approach such as that described above will serve as the basis or foundation for the shopping center security plan and all of its components. You should now be prepared to make logical, sound decisions on revising an existing security plan or in the development of a new safety and security plan.

A relatively inexpensive and basic crime deterrent concept that is frequently overlooked or not properly considered in the development of a security plan is the concept of Crime Prevention Through Environmental Design—CPTED.

Jon Lusher, Senior Vice President of IPC International, Bannockburn, Illinois, a frequent lecturer concerning the application of CPTED, provided the following commentary:

A key component of both the *perception* and *reality* of security at the shopping center is the physical property itself. Recognizing that the desirable users (customers, tenants and employees) have exactly opposite *perceptions* from the undesirable user (criminals, hangers-on) helps us to design and build facilities that encourage the former while discouraging the latter. For instance, customers prefer brightly lit parking lots, while criminals would prefer the dark.

In order to capitalize on these differences, the use of Crime Prevention Through

Environmental Design, or CPTED, is a critical tool. CPTED encourages us to design and build the shopping center so as to reduce the *reality* of crime and to improve the *perception* of safety and improve the quality of life at the center.

The six basic principles of CPTED help us understand how to accomplish these goals:

1. Natural Surveillance. Simply put, open, transparent and clear construction makes people feel safer and reduces opportunity for crime. Choosing materials and designs that allow for visibility is always preferable.
2. Access Management. There are certain places some people do not belong, and others we encourage people to use. Designing parts of our centers to discourage teen hangouts will improve the management of their behavior.
3. Territoriality. We should design space so that we know who "owns" it. Without this definition, space is often used by the undesirable user. It is critical to remember that within the center space may "belong" to tenants, employees, customers or the mall. No space should belong to more than one group; when there is confusion over whose space is whose, that space often is taken over by those whom we don't want to use it.
4. Maintenance. Shopping center professionals already know how important it is for the center to look like someone cares.
5. Order Maintenance. Security professionals already know that keeping order is paramount for *perception* and *reality*.
6. Activity Support. A busy center is safer than an empty one; keeping desirable users coming to the center for a variety of uses helps both *perception* and *reality*.

In applying these principles, a critical method involves Definition, Designation and Design. That is, each space must be Defined as to its use, Designated to serve that use and then Designed to support it. For example, we Define an entry by its location and character, we Designate it by signage and lighting, and then Design it to look like an entry. All too often, the entry becomes a hangout because one of these three D's hasn't been in phase with the others. If the Design of an entry encourages hanging out rather than use as an entry, the other two D's become dysfunctional. The result is that the space encourages the undesirable user, while discouraging the desirable one—both *perception* and *reality* suffer. Remembering that all spaces must have all three concepts in place will make that space usable for its intended users, and not for criminals or other undesirables.

CPTED also has as a basic premise that *perception* and *reality* are virtually indistinguishable. Thus, any argument about whether good lighting actually prevents crime is immaterial to the decision whether to upgrade lighting. In fact, CPTED emphasizes the *quality* of lighting rather than its amount; different areas call for different kinds of lighting. The Three D's would dictate, for instance, that parking areas in a garage would have different lighting than the areas where pedestrians walk in the same garage.

CPTED is not a mystical or magical cure for problems, nor can it be ignored in planning security for your center. It integrates perfectly with the use of video surveillance (enhancing natural surveillance with electronic surveillance), as well as with the use of personnel to maintain order and to help designate space. Furthermore, as a recognized component of security planning, the use of CPTED strategies is crucial for risk and liability management.

4 | Reality—A Security Officer Requirement

Through our "Step One" study we scientifically and systematically gained an understanding of the risks and potential threats to our property. As we progressed through the steps of this study, we should have become more aware of the many factors that may influence decisions related to the composition of the property security plan. We should now be prepared to answer a series of questions such as: Should we install fencing or other perimeter barriers? Is our parking lot signage effective? Do we need to supplement or improve parking lot lighting? Will access controls at identified doorways or loading docks be required? Have we developed reasonable emergency response plans?

Some identified safety and security risks may be minimized with the installation of hardware or management controls, while others may lend themselves to a physical security presence. If it is determined that officer presence is required, there are six (6) basic options to consider:

➢ Dedicated security staff—Proprietary (full or part-time)
➢ Dedicated security staff—Contractor (full or part-time)
➢ Shared contract security—part-time
➢ Off-duty police officer—part-time
➢ Special arrangement with police or sheriff for periodic patrols (part-time)
➢ Police substation on property (full time or part-time)

You may determine that any one or a combination of these security operations is suitable for your center's needs. There is no specific formula such as number of stores, measure of retail and/or common area space, acres of parking or sales volume that leads to a clearly defined security requirement. The exact composition of your function should be dictated by the results of your "First Step" study.

If you determine a need for, or have, a dedicated security staff, proprietary or contractor, full-time or part-time, it is important to understand that the staffing, organization, and operation of the security department are very important factors in the effectiveness of the security plan.

Since the security staff is typically the first, and most recognizable, group of mall representatives to meet customers (*reality*), tenants and vendors coming onto the property, it is important to properly select, train, staff and uniform the security department members. This initial impression of security is highly important to the customers and tenants alike since it sets the tone for the level of security that may be expected at the property (*perception is reality*). From a business standpoint, this is very important. A customer who feels safe and secure is likely to return, and he/she is likely to discuss this *perception* with others. Potential troublemakers are equally as likely to feel uncomfortable and go elsewhere to engage in disruptive or criminal behavior. They too will spread the word to others about their experience at your center. (*Perception Is Reality Concept*)

A staff trained in oral and written communication skills, security systems (hardware), and security operations is likely to function at a high level in maintaining order and safety. More and more the role of the security officer in a mall setting has increased in importance in terms of public *perception*, liability, customer service, and public and police relations. We know that many civil court actions are brought on the theory that property owners and managers failed to provide a reasonable and adequate level of security for the public while on their property.

The creation and development of a professional security staff, in-house or contract, begins with the selection of personnel. It is important to hire the best available people through an interview process that evaluates candidates' appearance, communication skills (oral and written), experience, and background. Throughout the selection process it should be kept in mind that members of the security department will be protecting the company's assets, limiting liability and representing your center to its customers, tenants, visitors and the public.

The value of a strong training program cannot be overemphasized. To inadequately or improperly train a security staff is certain to diminish its performance level and may lead to undue liability exposure in matters emanating from charges of inadequate security at the property.

Carefully selected and well-trained personnel must be supervised by an experienced security professional or law enforcement officer. The security director should possess above-average leadership skills, interpersonal skills, common sense and good judgment, maturity, and professional bearing and have the ability to make good decisions quickly. He/she should have demonstrated ability to establish and maintain excellent relationships with community leaders, particularly in law enforcement, and with fire, safety and emergency response personnel.

It should be the goal of management, through the security officer unit, to properly staff and deploy personnel in a highly visible manner. It is extremely important that a clear message is delivered to potential criminals and/or troublemakers that your center will not tolerate criminal activity that threatens the shopping public or tenants in any way. In so doing, the customers, tenants, employees, vendors and general public will immediately develop a positive view of safety and security at the mall and will continue to return. All of this can be done in a highly professional manner that is acceptable to everyone. Respect must be gained without offending patrons or tenants.

We will be discussing the use of off-duty police officers at shopping centers later in this book ("Partnering with Police, Fire and Emergency Services"). Here, we will discuss issues related to the selection, hiring and supervising contract security providers. You may evaluate the pros and cons and determine whether a proprietary (in-house) or contract security function is best for you.

CONTRACT VERSUS PROPRIETARY SECURITY

A number of issues may be examined when making a determination regarding the kind of security officer presence that is best for your center. Obviously, cost is always a factor when making critical business decisions. In the past, cost of security may have been a key factor in determining the type of security to be provided. In today's world, because an effective, efficient and professional security function may be deemed a business advantage, cost may be balanced against operational effectiveness. Many businesses are more willing to spend more money on security for a higher quality of service. With this new philosophy, the cost-versus-business-value type of thinking brings a number of additional factors into play.

In recent years there has been an increase in use of contract security vendors. This increase is due, in part, to elevated performance levels of private security. Today, upper-level management of the better contract security providers consists of highly educated, experienced security professionals. These senior-level security executives provide a valuable infrastructure for their field operations. That having been said, it should not be expected that all private security vendors are likely to provide high-quality service.

In analyzing the issues of contract security services versus a proprietary security officer operation, consider the following:

➢ Hiring practices
➢ Hiring expenses—advertisement
➢ Training
    State licensing requirements for officers

➤ Human resource issues
➤ Corporate infrastructure
➤ Liability—indemnification
➤ Supervision/management
➤ Costs (uniforms and equipment)
➤ Quality control—audit and evaluation

Most, if not all, private security vendors will assure that they will do all of the hiring, provide necessary training and handle human resource issues as they unfold. Typically, private security vendors may provide an insurance policy that will, in theory, indemnify the property owner in the event of a premises security lawsuit that involves the actions of one of their officers. Contract security providers normally include a number of supervisors and/or account managers who may remain on-site. It is important that you examine the corporate infrastructure supporting field operations that will be provided by your security contractor.

Generally, security contractors work on a cost schedule that allows for 70% of contract to officer payroll, 20% for administrative costs and 10% profit. These percentages may vary depending on negotiations with their customer.

A complete and well-thought-out security provider contract will permit the customer to maintain control of many of the listed issues. It is not a good practice to use the generic security vendor contract that is typically offered by the contract company. Clearly, if you are inclined to outsource security, it is incumbent on you as a landlord/customer to completely and accurately address each of the areas of service you require. It is important that you specifically define hiring practices, training requirements, human resource services, levels of supervision and management, insurance requirements and expected levels of corporate support. In-house or retained counsel should be consulted in the preparation of any security services contract.

Because hiring practices and training are two of the core elements of any security operation, the following are recommendations that may be used as a guide or attachment to a private security contract. The listed practices and training outlines may be applied to contract or proprietary security operations.

SUGGESTED SECURITY OFFICER HIRING PRACTICES

PROPRIETARY OR CONTRACT

➤ Personal interview after review of formal written application.
➤ Pre-employment background investigation, including prior employment checks, criminal background check.

➢ Pre-employment drug test as a condition of employment.
➢ Verification of education and/or guard registration (where applicable).
➢ Verification of valid nonrestricted driver's license (where applicable).

The overall effectiveness of security officer personnel will, in large part, be a product of the selection process. It is important that security officer candidates be thoroughly interviewed and critically evaluated on a number of dimensions including, but not limited to, background, experience, maturity, oral and written communications skills, appearance and education. No single set of experiences or education assures that a candidate will be successful. Many different backgrounds are suitable and, in fact, desirable as you assemble a security staff.

You may want to give consideration to ensure that the security staff is ethnically diverse and generally conforms with the general population makeup of your community or market share. Competitive wage rates should be offered.

TRAINING RECOMMENDATIONS

PROPRIETARY OR CONTRACT

It is recommended that a formalized security officer-training program patterned after the New York State Security Guard Act, or similar state licensing program, be implemented to train each new security guard. Programs such as these are extremely important to ensure that each officer has been afforded an adequate level of instruction as he/she begins assignment at your center. Records regarding this and all other training should be maintained by the Director of Security to be produced as required in connection with potential premises security litigation.

A sample eight (8)-hour security officers pre-assignment training program may include the following topics:

- Introduction to your center (philosophy of center management and ownership) .... $1/4$ hr
- Role of Security Guard .... $1^{1}/4$ hrs
- Legal Powers and Limitations .... 2 hrs
- Emergency Situations (general) .... 1 hr
- Communications/Public Relations .... 1 hr
- Access Control (general) .... $1/2$ hr
- Ethics and Conduct .... 1 hr
- Review and Examination .... 1 hr

A sample security officers on-the-job training program may include the following topics among a number of others.

This training is over and above the basic pre-assignment program.

- Role of the Security Guard broken down by specific posts and responsibilities .... 2 hrs
- Legal Powers and Limitations interacting with loss control, tenants .... 2 hrs
- Understanding Critical Situations/Areas .... 1 hr
- Emergency Situations (site-specific) .... 1½ hrs
- Communications—oral, written, radio, management of aggressive behavior .... 1½ hrs
- Access Control (site-specific) .... 1 hr
- Ethics and Conduct .... 1 hr
- Interviewing .... 1 hr
- Report Writing .... 1 hr
- Review and Examination .... 1 hr

All training should be approved by the Director of Security; however, since the Director will have a number of additional duties and responsibilities, it is useful to have more than one person involved in the training process.

Trainers should have a minimum high school diploma (and preferably advanced education or training). They should be schooled in training techniques and have security experience. It is advisable to have the Director of Security, staff trainers and selected management staff members receive training on customer service. Topics within this session will assist in the development of a customer/tenant-friendly security unit. The considerable differences in Mall Security vs. Standard "watch guard" Security must be clarified from the outset in order to develop the proper security environment.

Centers requiring the use of a central communications or command and control center should consider that personnel selected to perform duties in the Command and Control Center possess better than average oral communication skills, a good command presence and a demonstrated ability to make good decisions quickly and while under some level of stress. Testing and evaluation for these traits may be undertaken during the hiring and pre-assignment processes. Because of the nature of their assignment, dispatchers may receive a minimum of eight (8) hours of additional training concentrated on the following:

- Radio and telephone communications
- Addressing Courtesy Call Box alarms
- Operation and use of the CCTV network and recording devices (if installed)
- Graphic User Interface (if installed)
- Response to Fire Control Enunciator Panel—Fire Communications
- Operation of all other equipment in the command and control center

- Use and maintenance of the Security Operations Log
- Police and fire communications
- Emergency operations

The following is a topical outline for advance security training that may be provided to all officers throughout the months following the initial hire.

OUTLINE

A. **Introduction**
   1. Background of private security
   2. What is a security officer?
   3. What does security provide?

B. **Role of Security Officer**
   1. Principles
   2. Duties
   3. Emergency Situations
   4. Deter, Detect, Report
   5. Indicators of Employee Theft

C. **Legal Powers and Limitations**
   1. Authority
   2. Penalties and Problems
   3. Common Law and Criminal Law
   4. Security Officer vs. Police Officer
   5. Support for an Arrest
   6. What is an offense? What is a crime? Felony—Misdemeanor
   7. When can a security officer effect an arrest? Private citizen?
   8. Arrest procedures—Use of Force

D. **Emergency Situations**
   1. Fires
   2. Explosions
   3. Bomb Threats
   4. Civil Disturbances
   5. Strikes and Riots
   6. Hazardous Materials Accidents
   7. Natural Disasters
   8. Medical Emergencies

9. Evacuations
10. Crimes in Progress

Communications and Public Relations

1. The Communications Process
2. Components Necessary for Effective Communication
3. Attitude
4. Knowledge of Duties
5. Prejudices
6. Listening Skills
7. Interpreting the Message
8. Nonverbal Communication

Access Control

1. Elements
2. Written Documentation
3. Threat Potential/Risk Analysis
4. Awareness of Conditions

Ethics and Conduct

1. Integrity
2. Code of Ethics
3. Benefits of Code
4. Unethical Conduct

REVIEW AND TESTING

ROLE OF THE SECURITY GUARD AT YOUR CENTER (SITE-SPECIFIC)

1. Exterior Patrol—related to specific exterior features
2. Interior Patrol—common area
3. Interior Patrol—theaters, food court, identified special locations
4. Interior Patrol—service corridors, rest room areas

5. Mobile Patrol —Bike Patrol
6. Patrol of loading dock areas
7. Interacting with customers, tenants, vendors
   Customer Service, Information, Emergency Assistance, Safety Control, Traffic Control, Crowd Control, First Aid, Criminal Conduct, Police & Fire Liaison

LEGAL POWERS AND LIMITATIONS

1. Interacting with Loss Control Officers (anchors), tenants re: shoplifting
2. Detention, Arrest—False Arrest—Miranda Warnings
3. Use of Force—Restraints (yes or no)—under what conditions
4. Authority as a private citizen

UNDERSTANDING CRITICAL SITUATIONS/AREAS

1. Threat Assessment—nature and degree of risk
2. Identification of Critical Areas
3. Identification of Critical Situations (persons)
4. Understanding Criminal Conduct
5. Emergency Situations

EMERGENCY SITUATIONS

1. Recognition and response
2. Identification of critical areas (site-specific)
3. Evacuation plan
4. Augmenting police and fire

COMMUNICATIONS

1. Radio Communications
2. Listening and Communicating with the Public
3. Report writing
   Detail, writing technique, who, what, when, where, how
4. Avoiding conclusions and opinions
5. Management of Aggressive Behavior—Confrontational Situations

ACCESS CONTROL

1. Access Control Systems
2. Key Control
3. Alarms—responses
4. Barriers and Gates

ETHICS AND CONDUCT

1. Sexual Harassment
2. Civil Rights and Human Relations
3. Unreasonable Searches and Seizures
4. Stereotyping
5. Cultural Diversity

Review and Testing

The three (3) *perceived* advantages of a propriety security officer function most commonly mentioned are (*This perception may or may not be valid*):

➢ a tailored training program
➢ a stable, loyal work force
➢ ability for closer supervision and performance evaluation

Those inclined to favor a proprietary security officer function feel that they are better able to devise and implement an officer training program specifically tailored for their individual needs. They feel that they can promptly modify and restructure training as experience and circumstance dictate. Some corporate shopping center professionals believe that contract employees perceive themselves as "outsiders" and don't completely "buy in" to their company or shopping center staff. This *perception* should and can be avoided by continually involving contract supervisors and managers in all aspects of shopping center operations. In every instance it is important to educate employees in the business and operational philosophy of your company. When dealing with contract employees this should not be overlooked.

A concern of proponents of proprietary security officer operations is that of officer "bench strength." Since it is not uncommon for officers to miss work for illness or personal reasons, it is important to have "bench strength" or substitute personnel who are knowledgeable of the facility, its operations and philosophy. It is beneficial to have your contractor train and prepare officer backups to become familiar with your particular property rather than drawing from a pool of officers working in the same community who have not received site-specific training.

Clearly the decision to hire a contract security provider or manage an in-house security function is a corporate or individual property manager's decision. In either case, properly structuring and managing the security operation will gain the desired result.

Security Contractor Selection & Evaluation
Preparing Request for Proposal (RFP)
Contractor Evaluation and Selection

Currently there are well over ten thousand (10,000) private security providers in business in the United States. Many of these vendors are small local companies with limited resources. Some contract security firms specialize in providing controls at entry points of private property such as office buildings and manufacturing facilities. Still others support semiprivate properties that require an admission fee or visitor pass such as hospitals, amusement parks, entertainment venues or aquariums. Shopping centers, plazas, and community centers are public-access properties that require a security function prepared to operate much like a community police department. Security officers patrolling in a public-access facility must regularly interact with the public in a wide variety of safety and security duties. It is important that you accurately specify the nature and use of your environment and the identified security needs as determined through your "First Step" process. Be sure to determine if the contractor(s) you are considering are experienced in serving public-access facilities such as shopping centers as opposed to private property facilities. Security operations in an open public-access facility like a regional shopping center are considerably more complex and demanding than a fixed-post access control officer at an office building. The bidders' list should consist primarily of contractors who are experienced in providing security operations at public-access facilities. It is advisable, therefore, to conduct your vendor search from within the shopping center industry.

After you have identified a suggested minimum of four (4) potential security providers, it will be necessary to prepare a Request for Proposal (RFP). The RFP should clearly state the specific security functions you require at your property. You may desire to list the types of patrols (mobile, foot, dispatch, etc.) and hours that you project. Since officers will need two-way radios and other equipment as they conduct patrols, this should be specified. Any and all of your expectations or requirements regarding the following should be spelled out in the RFP:

Personal Conduct	Appearance	Uniforms and Equipment
Training	General and Specific Duties	Public Relations
Reporting Requirements	Emergency Service [alarm response]	Supervision
Telephone Use	Insurance Requirements	Lease Enforcement
Officer Qualifications	Supervisor Qualifications	Licensing Requirements

An identical RFP should be sent to each identified security firm. Potential contractors should be given adequate time to review your requirements. They should be encouraged to visit the property to conduct their own analysis of physical security needs. A knowledgeable property staff member should accompany them to answer any questions they may have as they survey the property.

Note: This practice affords you the opportunity to evaluate the knowledge, experience and professionalism of the contract company's representative.

Qualified vendors should be given a deadline for the submission of their proposal and bid. Proposals should be reviewed for form and content. Submissions with spelling and grammatical errors or proposals with boilerplate language deliver an unsatisfactory message and may be indicators of the kind of performance you may expect from the contractor. Proposals that introduce logical, practical and innovative ideas or suggested modifications to your RFP may prompt further discussion and be indicative of an experienced contractor who will bring value to the property. At the conclusion of the proposal review, qualified contractors should be invited to your property for a final walkthrough and interview.

Contractors qualifying for the interview process should be required to demonstrate an above-average working knowledge of security operations at a shopping center and should provide references during the interview process for follow-up verification. When all of the preliminary contractor selection work has been completed and a final candidate chosen, contract negotiations may begin.

When all terms and conditions of the proposed service are understood and agreed upon, a detailed contract or operating agreement should be developed. The following is a guideline of topics that may be considered for inclusion in a contract for security officer services. Many of the same topics should be considered in the structure and management of a proprietary security officer function:

A. Contractor's Responsibilities
   a) Employees, employee issues (proper number, appearance, independent contractor)
   b) Legal compliance
   c) Material and workmanship; fiduciary duties

    d) Operating Manual
    e) Quality Control—Contractor Evaluation
    f) Operating Log and Records
    g) Accountability
    h) No subcontracting
    i) Uniforms and Safety Equipment
    j) Training
    k) Other Services
    l) Cooperation With Management And Other Contractors
B. Representation of the Contractor [services]
C. Insurance Issues
D. Financial Reporting Responsibilities
E. Payment By Owner/Manager
F. Conditions of/for Termination

Exhibits (specifications) detailing hiring practices, officer qualifications, officer appearance/grooming standards, duties and responsibilities, hourly bill rate, training outline, etc. may be attached to any contract to assure the level of service is as expected. Avoid using "general" language. Precise and detailed agreements are notably easier to administer.

CONTRACTOR EVALUATION

It is important to include language in the security service contract that mandates continuous review and evaluation of security operations at the property. One way of creating an ongoing review and evaluation process is to require that the security director or manager create a weekly review of officer activity along with remarkable incidents, events or occurrences. This report is submitted to property management for further review and/or action that may be required. This practice keeps management appraised of security activity on a timely basis and may indicate an immediate need for operational adjustments, schedule changes or staffing and deployment modifications. This, or a similar custom, allows management to consistently evaluate security staff and officer performance.

In addition to a continuing review and evaluation process, it is helpful to conduct periodic full-scale safety and security audits or evaluations. These examinations may be conducted by in-house security professionals or a retained security consultant. Audits and evaluations such as these are designed to determine the effectiveness of the safety and security function as well as validate the overall security plan. The frequency of a full-scale security audit is largely dependent on the size of the property and the volume and nature of activity. The administration and costs related to these services should be clearly spelled out in the security services contract.

It is advisable to establish similar continuous and periodic review and evaluation procedures for a proprietary security function.

STAFFING AND DEPLOYMENT METHODOLOGY

PROPRIETARY OR CONTRACT

Once it has been determined that a property requires a physical security presence, it is necessary to identify the number and location of security posts or patrols to be manned. Since the volume of customer and vehicular traffic at a large retail environment changes relative to the time of day, day of the week and season of the year, the number and location of security posts or patrols is likely to change as well. The same factors impact scheduling of an in-house or contract security function at a shopping center.

Staffing and deployment of security officers at a plaza, strip center, community center or a shopping center is commonly based on incident type, frequency and location experienced or projected at your property. Experience tells us that approximately forty-five percent (45%) of all security incidents occur Friday—Sunday at a large super-regional shopping center. Of that percentage the highest rate, approximately fifty-six percent (56%), occur between the hours of four (4:00) PM and midnight. Typically, the highest concentration of activity during Friday through Sunday occurs at or near food courts and theaters. Most centers require that tenants remain open until nine (9:00) PM. With the exception of theaters, amusement centers, entertainment venues and restaurants, the activity at most shopping centers drastically decreases after traditional shopping hours. This predictable reduction of patrons and automobiles may allow management to proportionately reduce the security officer presence. At most private, semiprivate and public-access properties, during the late evening and early morning hours when there is little activity on the property, many posts are expanded or consolidated, requiring fewer officers to patrol within the same boundaries. Reducing officer staff, however, should not be based solely on reduced activity (*Reality*). Shared parking garages or lots that remain open and active for late evening use by nearby attractions may require special patrol consideration. It is advisable to clearly communicate security responsibilities with those sharing the parking facility.

After having identified the required posts of duty and the projected hours of active duty for each post, you, or the contract security company, can prepare a weekly security officer schedule. It is not advisable to regularly schedule officers for more than eight (8) consecutive hours or more than forty (40) hours of duty per week. Undoubtedly there will be times when, because of illness, personal emergencies or other extenuating circumstances, officers may be called upon to extend their tour of duty. This is understandable and acceptable. Regular and consistent over-scheduling may lead to officer fatigue and human error.

Regardless of whether you manage a proprietary or contract security operation, once a schedule has been set and officers have been deployed, it is a good practice to regularly monitor officer activity (volume and nature) with an eye toward modifying or adjusting staffing or deployment relative to days of the week, hours of the day, location on the property, and season of the year. This constant review may be beneficial from a security effectiveness standpoint as well as an economic advantage.

Staffing and deployment plans for special events should be handled on the basis of the size and type of event. Security operation issues related to special events is discussed in detail in the chapter entitled "Patrol Techniques and Procedures."

Once it has been determined that a security officer presence is required at your property, whether proprietary or contract, full-time or part-time, it should be made clear that the staffing, organization, operational supervision and administration of a physical security function are paramount in the overall effectiveness of the security plan.

THE ROLE OF THE SECURITY OFFICER

In the 1950s, homeowners and merchants appreciated the visibility and approachability of the neighborhood foot patrolman. Back then, officers were known to the people of the neighborhood and the people knew them, if not by name, by sight. They took comfort in knowing that Officer McNamara noticed them and became familiar with their daily routine. This presence of a symbol of public safety reassured the law-abiding public that they and their neighborhood were under the watchful eye of an officer. This consistent appearance of the neighborhood patrolman also sent a message to would-be perpetrators not to attempt criminal activity in or about the area.

Ideally, shopping center customers and property managers would be equally as pleased and comforted if, when a patron came to the shopping center, he/she observed a security vehicle patrolling the parking lot or a security officer acknowledged them as they entered the common area of the mall. Today, as in the 1950s, patrons, merchants, employees and vendors take comfort in observing and knowing that a public-access property has a physical security presence. There should be no doubt that the security officer, properly dressed in a recognizable uniform, typically is the first and most identifiable representative of the property. When we consider the role of the security officer and his mission at a shopping center or plaza, that initial visibility and recognition becomes extremely meaningful to staff, management and the shopping public.

A generic mission statement for security guards may be to deter, observe, detect and report unusual activity or incidents that occur on the property. Unlike the night watchman/security guard of yesteryear, today's shopping center security officer is charged with a much broader spectrum of duties and responsibilities. The shopping center security officer may be likened to the neighborhood foot patrolman of yesteryear without the legal powers. He/she should have above-average oral and written communication skills since officers are commonly called upon to interact with customers, merchants and vendors. The nature and use of most, if not all, shopping centers demands that security officers assist customers, merchants, vendors, policemen, firemen, emergency service personnel and vehicle operators on a daily basis. The following is a listing of some of the major duties and responsibilities of security officers at shopping centers or plazas:

➤ Enforcement of property rules, regulations and procedures (normally displayed at entrances or prominently about the property)
➤ Attempt to deter loss or damage to customers, merchants, vendors and employees
➤ Customer, merchant, employee, vendor assistance
➤ Traffic flow and control
➤ Access control (related to specific areas)
➤ Property inspection and risk management
➤ Prevention and deterrence of criminal activity
➤ Management of emergency and life safety situations
➤ Liaison with police, fire and emergency services
➤ Crime awareness and crime prevention programs and training
➤ Incident reporting and analysis
➤ Use and application of specialized security and life safety equipment

While all properties may not require all of the above-listed duties and responsibilities, a large number of these services are required by many retail centers. By using the "First Step" methodology discussed earlier in this book, it can be determined which of the listed duties conform to your property.

Virtually every facet of our lives is controlled or regulated by rules, laws or social practices. These controls establish order or structure in our homes, workplaces and communities. Since shopping centers, plazas and community centers are public-access facilities designed to provide a pleasant experience for patrons as they move about the property, it is necessary to establish guidelines for all to observe. These rules create an orderly environment that can be enjoyed by customers, merchants, vendors and visitors to the mall.

In this regard, it is a good practice to publish and prominently display property rules for customers, tenants and vendors to see. A professionally designed poster [minimum of 20" x 30"] created in colors that attract attention clearly citing mall rules may be displayed at entrances, the food court and other points of convergence. Definitive rules send a clear message to all visitors that management is serious about maintaining a safe and comfortable environment for everyone to enjoy as they shop, dine or attend entertainment venues on the property. A positive introductory paragraph often serves as a reminder to all as to why property rules are necessary. Posted rules and regulations serve as a reference point for security officers as they go about the business of maintaining order on the property. Failure to comply with posted rules may serve as a basis for banning and subsequent criminal trespass.

An example of property rules and regulations is as follows: In order to provide a safe, secure and pleasant environment at XYZ Center, management requires your complete cooperation in complying with the rules of conduct to be observed by all patrons, employees and visitors:

The following activities are prohibited on mall property:
1. Loitering.
2. Any act which could result in risk of injury or harm to persons or property.
3. Use of obscene language or gestures, or wearing clothing displaying obscene words or phrases.
4. Trespassing in any area of the mall not designated a public area.
5. Standing in groups in such a manner as to cause inconvenience to others moving about the mall or blocking mall entrances, storefronts or fire exits.
6. Running, horseplay, throwing debris, disorderly or disruptive conduct.
7. Playing radios, CDs, tapes or musical instruments unless approved by mall management.
8. Possession or use of alcoholic beverages or illegal substances.
9. Use of skateboards, roller/in-line skates or bicycles on mall property.
10. Walking the concourse without shoes or shirt.
11. Defacing or damaging mall property.
12. Carrying a weapon of any kind.*

*Possession of any article defined as a weapon—legal or otherwise. Exception: federal, state or local law enforcement officers required to carry weapons while on duty.

13. Taking photographs of mall property, storefronts, displays or other areas without written permission of mall management.
14. Distribution of any literature without written permission of mall management.
15. Any act defined by federal, state or local statute or ordinance as constituting a criminal act.

Violation Of Any Of These Rules May Result In Expulsion From The Mall, Or Arrest
This Is A No Smoking Facility

Some properties provide security officers with cards [3″ X 4″] printed with property rules for officers to distribute as a reminder to persons violating any of the property rules.

While it is clearly management's decision whether or not to display property rules or provide printed cards for security officers, rules and regulations are necessary and serve as the foundation for many of the actions of security officers.

The 1950s neighborhood foot patrolman had many of the same public safety goals, objectives and duties as today's shopping center security officer; however, his actions were/are supported by and granted authority through state and municipal laws. The policeman had/has the authority to search, detain and arrest. It is at this point that the role of the security officer is unmistakably different from that of the police officer.

Examining the role of the shopping center security officer, we can break down his primary duties and responsibilities in the following categories:

1. General Security Tasks
2. Customer Assistance
3. Tenant & Loss Control Assistance
4. Mall Operations
5. Liaison

General Security Tasks

Within the category of General Security Tasks, security officers are called upon to maintain order, assuring that all persons occupying the property follow site-specific property rules. Officers are expected to deter and detect through highly visible patrols in and about the property. Their proactive random patrols serve to protect persons and property. Smoke, water, fire and intrusion alarms are routinely monitored. An integral part of officers' patrols is observation and reporting of any unusual activity or occurrence. Analysis of reported incidents or activity aids in establishing or adjusting staffing levels and positions of deployment. Whether in a plaza, community center or enclosed super-regional mall, exterior patrols are likely to involve some level of traffic control.

Customer Assistance

The customer assistance aspect of the shopping center security officer's role, if performed effectively, brings an added dimension to that of most security officer positions. As a result of their familiarity with the entire property, officers are able to provide valuable assistance to customers experiencing difficulty finding a particular store, eatery, entertainment venue or rest room. Officers may direct disabled patrons to the nearest elevator, electronic door or handicapped parking. Officers assigned to parking area patrols are frequently called upon to assist in locating misplaced customer vehicles. They may also assist patrons with lockouts, flat tires, dead batteries or minor car trouble by calling a local mobile car service or AAA.

Customers, merchants, vendors and employees who experience a medical emergency at the center typically seek out a security officer to contact emergency services. Some centers provide security officers with basic first aid training and/or training in the use of an AED.

It is not uncommon for officers to assist in reuniting lost children with their parents or adult supervisors.

The highest level of security customer assistance is a proactive approach to safety, security and risk management. Officers who alert customers of a spill or trip hazard or observe an unattended child playing on an escalator are acting responsibly and are acknowledged favorably for their proactive actions. Parking area patrol officers suggesting to customers that packages be placed in the trunk or out of view bring added value to security at a shopping center.

Clearly it is this aspect of the shopping center security officer's role that creates a business advantage to the landlord.

Tenant and Loss Control Assistance

Without question the highest volume of criminal activity at any shopping center, plaza or community center originates with tenants. Shoplifting, credit card fraud, bad checks, and purse snatches commonly occur within the confines of tenant space. While many department stores have loss control personnel and formalized shrinkage reduction programs, a large majority of retail tenants rely on young, inexperienced sales associates to protect against losses.

Unquestionably shopping center security officers are charged with the safety and security of the public in the common areas of the property. It is not the officers' duty to serve as loss control officers for tenants. Officers can, however, make themselves visible at the tenants' lease line as they perform routine patrols. Patrolling in this manner and, on occasion, speaking to sales personnel serves as a deterrent to criminal activity within tenant spaces. Larger security staffs periodically provide security tips to tenants in the form of a security newsletter or bulletin or through quarterly tenant meetings.

Some shopping center management companies have worked closely with their security providers, tenants and police to establish a crime alert program that incorporates a communication tree wherein all tenants are alerted to a group or individual who has victimized another tenant or tenants with a criminal scheme. While this program can be a very effective crime prevention and solution effort, extreme caution must be exercised to assure that accurate information is networked, avoiding misidentification of suspects. Security officers and tenants armed with inaccurate information may act inappropriately or irresponsibly, giving rise to adverse legal action against the landlord and/or security company.

Arguably no single area of mall security brings greater potential for civil litigation than security's interaction with mall shop tenants or anchor/department store loss prevention officers. While shoplifting is a serious security matter, it is primarily the retailer who must address this issue. It must be clearly explained and understood during the training process that security officers do not have the power of arrest or detention. Thus, when called upon by a tenant or loss prevention officer to detain a shoplifting suspect, officers must remember the extent of their authority. Unlawful detention for questioning or a search creates unnecessary exposure to civil action. Security officers must be trained to assist tenants in the identification of suspects and ask the suspect to remain for police. Suspects should never be searched by a security officer or at the direction of a security officer.

Mall Operations

Many of the security officers' duties and responsibilities in the category of mall operations are controlled by tenant lease language, property rules, and municipal and fire codes. Typically, by lease, tenants agree to open and close each day at specific times. In a shopping center setting, security officers are asked to monitor tenant opening and closing as they move about on routine patrol. Officers patrolling service corridors and/or tenant loading areas may be asked to insure that service corridors are free of obstruction (boxes and trash). Interior patrol officers should verify that tenant spaces are properly locked as they make their rounds after and before mall shopping hours.

It is common practice for security to control keys to roof access and utility and mechanical rooms. Since the events of September 11, 2001, many centers require that kind of security control access to loading docks. In some cases gated loading docks are opened by security personnel only after vendors are cleared through a tenant or the management office. Often open loading areas are the subject of patrol or equipped with intercom devices for drivers to identify themselves and the tenant to whom they are delivering.

Exterior patrol officers routinely check parking areas and customer walking routes for failed lighting. Lighting reports are forwarded to mall operations for correction. This and other risk management procedures will be discussed in greater detail elsewhere in this book.

Liaison

Since most public-access private properties are dependent on local police, fire and emergency services, it is necessary that shopping center security and management establish and maintain excellent relations with these agencies. Suggestions on how security and management may develop and enhance this relationship are contained in the chapter entitled Partnering with "Police, Fire and Emergency Services."

In accepting his/her role as a shopping center security officer, it is highly important that he or she constantly demonstrate honesty, courtesy, discipline and professionalism. Since he/she must constantly interact with customers, tenants, vendors, and police, fire and emergency service personnel, oral and written communication skills should be above average. The security officer's appearance is not only important to him/her but to the entire security staff and management. As the most recognizable and visible representative of the property, officer appearance leaves a lasting impression on all who observe him/her. The security officer's demeanor and bearing typically dictates the level of respect and cooperation he gains from people. For this reason, security officers are held to a higher standard as they conduct their daily tasks. Finally, shopping center security officers should regularly and consistently display a thorough understanding of their role in the overall effectiveness of operations at the property.

Having listed and explained the duties and responsibilities that make up the role of the shopping center security officer, we can clearly see how different he/she is from the "watchman" of yesteryear and how similar his role is to that of the neighborhood patrolman of 1950s. Much like the neighborhood patrolman, the security officer in a shopping center environment brings the elements of safety, security and comfort to customers, merchants, vendors and employees through his presence and high visibility as he/she goes about the business of performing all of the listed diverse tasks.

Obviously the more effective and efficient he/she is in performing these duties, the greater positive public recognition. If the public feels safe and secure, they will continue to return to the property and are likely to communicate their positive perception to friends, neighbors and relatives. When this occurs, the shopping center and its security function have created a value-added dimension to its business.

5 | The Reality of Security and the Law

It's the Christmas holiday shopping season at SuperCenter USA in a suburb of Chicago. Mall tenants' sales associates have been encouraged by management to park in remote parking locations, reserving the closer, more convenient spaces for customer parking.

At approximately 10:30 PM, after closing her store, Alice Smith walks through the center's parking lot to her car, where she is abducted and robbed by an unknown assailant. As Ms. Smith attempts to fight off her assailant, she sustains injuries to her head and upper body. She is hospitalized for several days and later requires psychological attention to relieve stress suffered as a result of the incident.

Some months later mall management is served with notice that, through her attorney, Ms. Smith has filed a civil action in county court alleging that SuperCenter USA failed to provide an adequate level of security at the property that would have prevented or deterred the incident in which she was assaulted and sustained physical and emotional injuries.

In the original complaint Ms. Smith claims, among other things, that there was inadequate lighting in the parking lot, security officers were improperly staffed and deployed, and she was directed to parking in a remote area of the parking lot. She claims that each of these factors singularly and collectively directly influenced the assault and robbery. She claims that mall management had a duty to provide for her safety and security.

While the above scenario is fictitious, it is one that could happen at any property at any time. Because our society has become more security-conscious, people expect higher levels of visible security in place to provide for their personal protection. If crime victims believe that existing security failed or was inadequate, there is little hesitancy in initiating a lawsuit to recover physical and emotional damages.

In his book entitled *A Complete Guide to Premises Security Litigation*, attorney Alan Kaminsky, with the law firm of Wilson, Elser, Moskowitz, Edelman and Dicker, New York, NY, describes a premises security lawsuit (also known as a negligent security lawsuit) as a claim for damages brought in civil court on behalf of a crime victim, usually against the owner of the premises where the crime occurred. The victim of a crime such as a mugging, assault, or rape seeks to hold the landowner responsible for the injuries—usually both physical and psychological—that the victim sustained, contending that the crime was "caused" by the landowner's failure to provide sufficient security to protect persons from criminal occurrences at the location.

Courts across the land have generally found that as an owner or manager of a shopping center or plaza, you have essentially invited or encouraged the public (patrons) to access your property. By virtue of this invitation or encouragement, the shopping center owner and/or manager has established a special relationship with his patrons that brings with it a duty to provide protection from the acts of a third party. To be sure, the exact level of protection that is considered adequate may vary drastically from one jurisdiction to the next. A number of other factors, including, but not limited to, location of the property, history of crime on the property and in the neighborhood, and the nature of the crime, may influence the court's determination regarding the adequacy or requirement for security at a given property.

For instance, if a patron is assaulted at a small plaza located in a suburban location with a low incidence of crime, and there had never been any crime on the property prior to the assault, it is likely that most courts would find that the plaza owner/manager had a duty to provide only a minimum level of security for its customers. The question still remains, what is a "minimum" level of security in that instance?

Courts across the country have been inconsistent in their rulings in many aspects of premises security cases, making it very difficult for property owners/managers to have a clear understanding of their security responsibilities and requirements.

Mr. Kaminsky identifies the basic elements of a premises security case that a plaintiff must establish:

- The defendant owed a duty to protect the injured crime victim
- The defendant breached that duty
- The breach of the duty was a proximate cause of the criminal act and the victim's injuries

We can see that "duty" is the foundation on which premises security matters are based. Given that shopping center owners/managers, in all probability, are likely to be found to have established a special relationship with their patrons, a prudent thinking person may logically conclude that there is a duty on the part of a shopping center owner/manager to provide some undefined level of security to his or her customers, employees and vendors.

While all of this thinking seems quite simple and straightforward and follows a logical progression, there is one additional legal element that typically enters the equation in a premises security lawsuit—*foreseeability*.

Many courts have found that without foreseeability there can be no duty; therefore, it is necessary for the plaintiff in premises security cases to establish that the landlord knew or should have known that the criminal act was likely to have occurred. This is commonly done by presenting evidence of prior crimes on the property or in the neighborhood. Some courts do not require that this evidence be of a similar crime.

It is important to have a basic understanding of the factors and elements that are involved in premises security litigation, for it is with that understanding that one can make reasonable decisions in establishing or evaluating security needs at a specific property.

Since there is no way to determine the precise level of security that a court may determine is adequate for your property, it is best to take the "Step One" approach (described earlier in this book) to understand your risks, threats and vulnerabilities. These factors may then be addressed with the following safety and security components:

➢ Directional and informational signage
➢ Lighting
➢ Technical and mechanical support
➢ Physical security presence

Since many premises liability lawsuits involving shopping centers originate in parking lots and garages and since most security plans are built from the outside in, it is wise to consider all exterior measures and controls that may minimize exterior criminal incidents or accidents.

Adequacy of exterior lighting frequently becomes an issue in both third-party criminal acts and pedestrian or vehicular accidents. It is wise to insure that existing lighting is bright, consistent and evenly distributed throughout the parking facility. Lighting should be inspected frequently and bulbs replaced promptly to minimize darkened areas in parking lots. If the parking facility (garage or lot) is equipped with a closed circuit television system, lighting should be satisfactory to support the system.

Consideration should be given to safety and informational signage throughout the parking lots. Such signage serves as a parking reference point for customers and reduces the chance that they will spend long periods of time wandering about the lot looking for their vehicle. Patrons roaming aimlessly about a parking lot are more likely to become crime or accident victims.

Informational signage affixed to light poles may include phrases such as:

➤ Note the column number of your parking space [ex. Blue 8]
➤ Remember to lock your car
➤ Avoid leaving valuables on car seats—put packages in your locked trunk
➤ Never leave small children unattended—don't let them roam the mall unsupervised

If you reasonably determine that your property requires an exterior physical presence, consideration should be given to placing officers in well-marked, high-visibility patrol vehicles. Bicycle patrols may also be effective and efficient in specific instances and temperate climates. Depending on the size and configuration of the parking facilities, it may be advisable to establish exterior patrol zones or beats for multiple vehicles or bikes.

If a closed circuit television system (CCTV) is a part of your exterior security package, you should not display signage indicating that the entire property or parking lot is under video surveillance. Any CCTV system should be regularly serviced and maintained to avoid litigation emanating from failed or improperly maintained camera equipment.

Trees and shrubbery on the perimeter of the property and within the parking lot(s) should be trimmed to allow for clear, open lines of sight and to minimize areas of cover and concealment for would-be perpetrators.

You should know that in a *tort* claim, the plaintiff alleges that a civil or private claim gives rise to legal liability. Typically *negligence* is cited. In layman's terms, negligence is omitting to do something that a reasonable man would or should have done under ordinary conditions. When used in conjunction with a premises security lawsuit, negligence refers to the owner/manager of the premises failing to use ordinary care to reduce or eliminate unreasonable risk of harm created by premises conditions that the landlord knew about or should have known about.

While no one wants, or expects, to be named as a defendant in a premises security lawsuit, the probability of that occurrence has increased in recent years. By taking the "Step One" approach and giving consideration to your legal "duty," you can now move to the interior of your center and make reasonable decisions on security measures and controls that go to make up an overall security package that is likely to withstand the scrutiny of the courts in the event your property has the unfortunate circumstance of having to defend itself in a premises security lawsuit. In this way you can avoid allegations of negligence.

The following is a listing of some issues commonly addressed in premises security matters that involve shopping centers:

• Basis and authority for your security plan
  Is it updated regularly—by whom—on what basis?
• When was the last security review or audit?
  Produce documentation

- Where does security fall in your organizational chart?
  Does the Security Director or Manager participate in management-level meetings, budget planning sessions?
  By what means do you communicate critical incidents to management?
  How timely is the reporting?
- Is your center a part of a management group?
  Is there uniformity among the group regarding security policies, procedures and practices?
- Who is the on-site security manager?
  What are his/her qualifications? Advanced training (documented)—experience—previous experience?
- Who comprises the physical security force?
  Number of full and part-time officers—pre-employment background—testing—qualifications—work experience—education—salary vs. other staff people
- What site-specific pre-employment training were officers given (documented)?
- What is the level of officer familiarization with security policy, procedure and post orders?
- Do you have a security manual?
  When was it last updated? Are officers required to sign off after reading the manual? (produce documentation)
- Are daily logs maintained? By whom? Who receives a copy? Who acts on review?
- Do guards maintain daily activity reports? Who reviews them? What types of activities are recorded?
- How visible are security officers? Produce a photo of an officer in uniform. Does he display a badge? Wear a hat? What equipment does he carry? Is he licensed? Is he/she certified according to state requirements?
- How visible is the patrol vehicle or bicycle? Is the vehicle/bicycle equipped with insignia, emergency bar lighting, two-way radio?
- What is the relationship to local police? Regularity of meeting? Sharing of statistics? Shared communications? Common training drills (on-site)? Are off-duty officers used? Is the center regularly patrolled by local police? Does the center have a police substation?
- Is there a security awareness program in place for tenants and staff?
- Do you maintain records of tenant complaints regarding safety and security? Are there tenant meetings addressing security issues? How do you communicate security issues to the tenants? Is there a tenant watch program?
- Are mall rules prominently posted?
- Do you maintain logs reflecting maintenance of shrubbery, traffic control signage, parking lot surface repair? (maintenance of security vehicle, CCTV, access controls, alarms, fencing)

- Do you perform lighting surveys (documentation)?
- How do you determine security officer staffing and deployment? Are shifts staggered? Do you maintain records of staffing and deployment? Do you have 24-hour security presence?
- What security systems do you have in place? (guard tour system, CCTV, fencing, access control, parking lot patrols, emergency call boxes)
- Is your security function a member of any security organization? (records of attendance at seminars/conferences) Do you subscribe to any security publications?
- What is the security budget as a percentage of the total budget?
- How do you identify "hot" or potential trouble areas on the property?
- Do you have any special security procedures at or near ATMs or with respect to bank courier services?

While this list may not be all-inclusive and may not be applicable to all shopping centers, plazas, strip centers, or community centers, it should serve as a guide in establishing reasonable and appropriate security operations at your property.

In many instances of premises security litigation involving shopping centers, the properties had reasonable and adequate security measures and controls in place at the time of the incident but are unable to document their performance. For this reason, it is prudent to create potential litigation folders when a critical incident occurs on the property. A potential litigation folder should contain any and all documents that serve to demonstrate the property management's performance at the very time of the occurrence of the incident.

In the event of a critical incident on property, collect and preserve the following—

- ➢ Photographs (current—as soon as possible after the incident)
- ➢ Leases for all tenants
- ➢ Contracts with security-related services (guards, locksmiths, security device companies)
- ➢ Current site plan—floor plan
- ➢ Complete tenant list (define each tenant's business)
- ➢ All records documenting inspection, maintenance and repair (six months prior to incident)
- ➢ Listing of all security measures in place (locks, access control devices, CCTV, alarm devices, etc.). Records of repair and maintenance of these items.
- ➢ Tenant complaints—memoranda or minutes re: tenant meetings, particularly concerning security issues and their resolution
- ➢ Prior security audits or surveys

- CCTV tapes, alarm printouts, guard tour records, access control records (time of entry and person accessing)
- Parking controls—related records
- All records relating to security guard performance—staffing, deployment, inspections, observations, incident reports, officers' post orders, guard company's policies and procedures, hiring and training requirements
- Reports of *all prior incidents* [three (3) years preceding incident]
- Records of police calls for service to the property [three (3) years preceding incident]
- Police report and investigative file re: incident (as it becomes available)
- Copies of newspaper articles relating to the incident
- Listing of witnesses to the incident (include DOB, address, etc.)
- Listing of all company or contract employees working on site at the time of the incident
- Listing of all maintenance, janitorial and service personnel regularly working at the site
- Copy of security plan for the property
- Copy of emergency management and building evacuation plan
- Records relating to due diligence in the purchase of the property (security-related)
- Local building codes or fire codes relating to ingress and egress
- Letters, memoranda, and invoices relating to security plans, repairs or purchases
- Memoranda, pamphlets or publications related to security or security awareness that may have been distributed to the tenants or provided with the lease
- Records of any special arrangements with tenant(s)

Copies of all records should be maintained in a "potential litigation file" (Not necessarily captioned as such)

While the above list may not be all-inclusive for every type of critical incident that may occur on the property, it should serve as a guide to reconstructing circumstances prior to and at the time of a given incident.

In short, it is wise to preserve anything that will document center operations at the moment in time the incident occurred. A potential litigation file may be maintained until your legal advisor(s) determines it is safe to discard.

The attitude that liability insurance is carried to provide protection from these type cases is not well-founded. To be sure, there are many other costs associated with such lawsuits that may have an adverse effect on your center, not the least of which is the cost of re-marketing your property in the event of a highly publicized nasty incident.

The previous pages of this chapter are not designed to make you an expert on premises security litigation. They are meant to provide a basic working knowledge of broad legal issues you may consider in developing a new security plan or evaluating a current operation. By gaining a basic familiarity with some of the elements of a premises security lawsuit, you may be better positioned to insure that your security plan has the necessary components and functionality to minimize your risk of becoming a defendant in such a suit. Further, in the event you are named as a defendant in a premises security matter, you may be better positioned to successfully defend your property.

6 | Partnering with Police, Fire and Emergency Services

Whether you are a large super-regional shopping and entertainment center located in a densely populated suburb or a community center located in a more moderately populated community, it is important to establish a working relationship with the local police and emergency services agencies. Typically the number and type of tenants in a center will dictate the market share and how far that market reaches from the center. The market share radius (from the center) is likely to shrink in urban areas; however, because of the population density, a high volume of patrons is likely to consistently visit the center. In the instance of more moderately populated suburban areas, customers may be traveling from longer distances to shopping centers and predictably spend more time on the property per visit. In either case, shopping centers, plazas, and community centers annually host large numbers of customers at their property. They are truly the downtowns of yesteryear. Commonly these attractive and convenient retail centers have a higher volume of pedestrian and vehicular traffic than any other single location in a community. With these higher volumes of people, it can be expected that there may be an increased probability of personal accidents, medical emergencies, and other safety and security incidents. With this in mind, you should understand that property management is likely to depend on police, fire and emergency services on a regular basis. Therefore, it is important to establish a good working relationship with them. Police, fire and emergency services administrators look upon the shopping center environment in different ways. Listed are some of the attitudes or positions that may be encountered in dealing with them:

➢ The mall is a drain on manpower.
➢ We are called to the mall for far too many minor incidents that should have/ could have been resolved by security or management.

➢ False or defective burglary, robbery and fire alarms originating at the mall are troublesome.

➢ The mall should pay us (fire, police) for additional manpower, services and equipment required to respond to their needs.

➢ We can't provide a higher level of services to the mall when other businesses are complaining of lack of services. (It is this attitude that hinders placement of a police substation within a shopping center or community center)

➢ Incidents at the mall are a drain on the overall effectiveness of our department's operation.

➢ Many of the mall's patrons are not members of our community. We are essentially providing police protection and emergency services to a regional population.

➢ Because the mall draws from many miles around, it draws higher levels of crime, youth problems and the like that we don't have in our community.

➢ The shopping center is an integral part of our community. It is our job to provide adequate services to our citizens.

It is easy to understand how many police and emergency services agencies may develop some of the negative attitudes reflected above. To be sure, many of them are valid.

An important part of establishing a good working relationship with police, fire and emergency services is having a clear understanding of their attitudes and what may have triggered or developed this posture.

INITIATING A GOOD WORKING RELATIONSHIP

Just as you would have marketing and demographic data available to you when talking to a prospective tenant, it is advisable to have a complete safety and security information package available to you prior to arranging a meeting with the police, fire or emergency services. The information you have compiled should be used to insure that you have a solid working knowledge of what is occurring (or likely to occur) at your center. Police, fire and emergency services may find it interesting and useful to know that you are tracking and trending incidents at the property; however, do not use your incident data to refute or contest their "calls for service." You may decide at some future date to do a statistical comparison. Avoid becoming confrontational. Listen!

Try to arrange your first meeting(s) with the police chief, fire chief, and lead emergency services person. During the first meeting, make it clear that it is your purpose to establish an improved (or new) working partnership with each of the service providers, aimed toward developing the most effective and efficient use of manpower and services. Determine who should be the point of contact for future meetings and if that person will be given authority to effect identified and necessary changes.

It is important for you to listen to all of the issues the agencies have in providing service to your property. Determine if they have recommendations or reasonable resolutions to their issues. Inquire as to how they feel your safety and security function may be helpful in resolving or minimizing their issues. Ultimately it should be everyone's goal to understand that a shopping center, plaza, strip center or community center is a community attraction and that it brings possibly the largest gathering of people to any single location in that community. It is for this reason that police, fire and emergency services should be encouraged to partner with the property's safety and security operation to insure the public's safety.

COMMON ISSUES TO ADDRESS WITH POLICE, FIRE, AND EMERGENCY SERVICES

There are a number of common issues that typically need to be addressed as a shopping center creates, enhances or develops a solid partnership with police, fire and emergency services. Some of these issues are:

- Traffic control at entrances and exits, particularly during holiday season
- Banning and trespassing—enforcement issues
- Unnecessary calls for police assistance
- False alarms—burglary, fire, smoke, water flow
- Establishing urgency codes associated with the type of incident
- Regularity/frequency of exterior police patrols at the property
- Establishing a police/fire or emergency services substation on the property

Oftentimes local codes, regulations and practices may affect the eventual resolution of these issues. It should be kept in mind that there is no "one size fits all" when developing police, fire and emergency services relationships.

USE AND SUPERVISION OF OFF-DUTY POLICE OFFICERS

Many property owners and/or managers determine that it is advantageous to use off-duty police officers to augment their security operation. Off-duty officers are typically hired to work during the busy Friday evenings, Saturdays and Sundays.

The specific hours and length of time off-duty officers are used is the decision of property management and is typically based on incident history and the volume of customers visiting the center during specific time periods and on identified days. A number of issues should be considered and/or discussed with the officers and their department relative to the use of off-duty officers.

1. Are the officers hired as independent contractors and paid as such, or are they hired as special "detail" officers with payment to the police department for subsequent distribution? Note: *Special detail officers working under the direction of a police superior may be covered by their department's worker's compensation plan.*
2. Will officers carry sidearms as they patrol the mall? This may be dictated by department policy.
3. Can you hire a single officer, or does the department dictate that two officers are hired for any given tour? Can the officers patrol independently, or does the department dictate that patrols are done in twos?
4. Do police officers, acting in an off-duty capacity, have full police powers? Most states consider that police officers are on duty 24 hours per day. *This issue should be clarified at the outset.*
5. Do you want police officers to effect arrests on the spot, as necessary, when working for the property?
6. Will you provide off-duty officers with post orders or a briefing associated with their detail? *Recommended practice.*
7. What process is in place to assure that the off-duty officer performs to the required level? *This is best handled by a superior officer in the officer's department.*

If the decision is made to use off-duty police officers, it is advisable to establish, in writing, your expectations of the officer or officers at the outset of hiring them. If the officer(s) is hired through the department as a special detail officer, this can be done through the supervisor of special detail officers. In this instance it should be determined that all complaints concerning the officer's performance while working at your center can be directed to the officer's supervisor.

It is advisable to provide officers that are hired as independent contractors with a detailed set of performance guidelines that include, but may not be limited to, appearance requirements, wage and benefits structure, general duties, and property-specific policies and procedures.

In either case, it is a good practice to provide off-duty officers with regular briefings regarding specific areas of concern or recent incidents. Even though he/she is a police officer, when he/she is working as an off-duty hire, he/she is your employee when enforcing property rules and should take direction from your designated security person.

Since it is not always clear who is responsible for any potentially negligent acts of an off-duty police officer on your property when he is hired by a private property owner, it is highly possible that the owner/landlord and the police department may be held responsible for such acts, particularly if an injury results. Further, there may be instances where the police officer is personally held liable if he is grossly negligent and/or is found to have acted outside the scope of his employment. The close association that exists between parties when off-duty police officers work closely with private security makes it difficult to clearly distinguish when the officer was acting privately (at the direction of property management) or when he was performing public officer duties.

Because of the inherent risks in hiring off-duty police officers to augment your physical security presence, it is advisable to enlist the aid of legal counsel in drafting a contract that clearly defines the officer's duties and responsibilities when working at your center. The contract should also address worker's compensation issues in the event of officer injury. While any such contract may not completely eliminate liability on the part of the landlord, it will help the officer, and his department, understand the conditions of the officer's off-duty employment with your center.

POLICE, FIRE OR EMERGENCY SERVICES SUBSTATION

The concept of police substations at shopping centers, plazas, strip centers and community centers has become popular in many communities throughout the country. As previously discussed, most regional or super-regional shopping centers and entertainment complexes become the center of much community activity. It is safe to say that upwards of ten million (10,000,000) people frequent many of these facilities on an annual basis. For this reason, and because of the centralized location of many shopping center properties, it is favorable to establish a police and/or fire substation on the property. Such an arrangement permits the police, fire or emergency services department to quickly respond and address safety and security incidents at the mall in addition to occupying a high-visibility community relations location.

A police, fire or emergency services substation, or any combination of these services, should be situated in a space that is clearly visible to mall patrons and should be tastefully signed with the name of the department(s). If possible it is advisable to have the space constructed with a partial glass storefront looking on to the common area. For security and operational reasons, a rear entrance providing access to a service corridor or directly to the parking facility is suggested.

Substation equipment may include the following:

- telephone with direct line capability to the mall security control center
- fax machine

- police department radio equipment—communications to headquarters
- computer terminal linked to PD network
- photo and fingerprint equipment
- CCTV monitors with switching capability
- desks and chairs
- built in workstation (reception area)—for CCTV monitoring (where applicable), communications, report writing, computer monitor and keyboard

It may be suggested that officers assigned to the substation carry out one or more of the following functions:

- process shoplifters or perpetrators of other criminal acts on property
- community policing from the storefront
- assist in tenant crime prevention programs
- periodically patrol the mall interior
- liaison with mall security director re: special issues/events
- periodic fire safety inspections
- fire safety and emergency procedure exhibits

In conjunction with the substation, the police, fire and/or emergency services department can be provided a reserved parking space in a nearby location in the parking facility for their vehicle(s).

7 | Role of the Security Function

Because it is difficult, if not impossible, to quantify the value of the security function in the shopping center environment, security has been looked upon as a necessary expense, not a profit center. Unquestionably, it is impossible to measure what did not happen. It is problematic to envision the economic impact that a non-event would have had on your center or your company had it occurred. By effectively doing their job of deterring crime, managing safety risks, protecting assets, and providing a safe and secure environment for customers, employees and merchants, security has succeeded in blocking out its true value. Historically, since the security function has been looked upon by management as not having any real value, in many instances it has been buried well below upper-level management in the organizational structure.

Listed below are the areas of the shopping center's operations that typically partner with security on a regular basis. This list is provided to assist management in gaining a greater knowledge and appreciation of the security function as an integral part of shopping center management:

1. customer, merchant and employee security
2. customer, merchant and employee safety (risk management)
3. mall operations (maintenance, housekeeping, janitorial, engineering)
4. tenant compliance
5. shipping and receiving
6. public/community relations
7. finance and insurance
8. sales
9. protection of physical and business assets

In reviewing this list, you may find that security could be the single function among the center's staff that regularly interacts with every department in the shopping center organization. Each of the listed areas has risks and vulnerabilities that can and should be evaluated and addressed by an effective security function.

Customer, merchant and employee security—needs begin when the center opens for business. The security function is charged with providing a safe, secure, and comfortable shopping and work environment for all who come onto the property.

Customer, merchant and employee safety—again it is security that must be vigilant in its risk management responsibilities to help prevent/avoid accidents and resulting claims.

Mall operations—security regularly performs parking lot lighting surveys and monitors smoke and water flow valves and mechanical rooms. Security must interact with janitorial, housekeeping and maintenance staff to insure that safety hazards are removed or minimized.

Tenant compliance—lease language specifies hours of operation, lease line restrictions and many other items. These items are typically monitored by security.

Public and community relations—clearly, security personnel are the most visible and interactive of the mall staff. Their customer service, tenant assistance and liaison with police, fire and emergency services sets them up as key public and community relations representatives of the mall.

Finance and Insurance—most insurance companies regularly send risk management representatives to large accounts such as malls to inspect the property for undue safety hazards and safety compliance. It is the security function in partnership with mall operations that interacts with the insurance risk manager to insure that corrections are made. Continuous failure to remedy identified risks may result in increased premiums, therein affecting company profits.

Sales—undeniably sales volume at the center is likely to be higher if patrons come in large numbers and stay for extended periods of time. This is more likely to occur if customers feel that they are in a safe and secure environment; this is a by-product of effective security.

Protection of Physical and Business Assets—the very foundation of any shopping center, plaza or community center is the physical assets of the center. One of the primary purposes of establishing a security function is to protect company assets. It should not be forgotten that a company's reputation and standing in the community are also assets to be protected by the security function.

In viewing security's total partnership with the entire shopping center staff, and the now quantifiable value that is achieved, strong consideration should be given to include security management among the upper level of the shopping center organization chart. When the center's security manager or director has reporting responsibilities directly to the property manager, critical incidents and occurrences and upcoming events are addressed promptly and in accordance with management's overall business plan. This arrangement makes it far easier for upper-level management to work more efficiently with security on traditional problem areas such as budget, personnel and training, legal and coordination of services. When the security manager is directly responsible to the property manager he/she will be prone to require a high level of performance from his/her staff since he/she is held directly responsible to the property manager for any safety and security deficiencies that are identified. From a premises liability standpoint, having the security manager/director as part of the management team, directly reportable to the property manager, bodes well toward property management's recognition of the value of safety and security on the property.

8 | Security Officer vs. Police Officer

In examining the roles, duties and responsibilities of the private security officer and the "public" police officer, we find that the two have much in common. Both the police officer and the private security officer are charged with protection of persons, places and things (buildings and/or assets) and maintaining order. While the "public" police officer derives his authority from state, local or municipal law, the private security officer's limited authority comes from the common law, or that of a private citizen, some local statutes and the rules, policies and procedures of his employer. Although the basic mission of public and private officers is very much the same, the level of authority and specific services provided are notably different.

Since police officers are sworn and warranted by the municipality in which they work and are given a higher level of authority under which to operate, they are charged with the prevention and regulation of serious criminal conduct. Without the higher level of authority granted to the police officer, private security can monitor and regulate only noncriminal conduct that may occur on their property. It is through operational deterrence and detection that security officers may prevent crime or observe and report a criminal action for police response.

CITIZEN'S ARREST

In most states, citizens may effect an arrest when they physically observe or witness another party committing a felony—citizen's arrest. A private citizen may not arrest another party who has committed a misdemeanor except where local law provides for special provisions. One of the common exceptions to misdemeanor arrest limitations may be found in the local business law of many states that permits a retail merchant or their employee to arrest for shoplifting as a misdemeanor (for example, Section 218, New York General Business Law). Unmistakably, this exception applies to merchants and does not grant any such authority to security officers. This exception does not exist in all states or municipalities.

Since security officers typically act under the direction and authority of the property owner/manager, they are likely unable to effect an arrest unless a felony is committed in their presence. A private security officer's authority is usually comparable to that granted to a common citizen. In some states or jurisdictions, security officers are granted "special police powers" by virtue of a special arrangement with the local policing agency or through the state licensing procedure. Under this provision of a higher level of authority, the power of arrest may be included but is restricted to the property on which the security officer functions.

SEARCH AND SEIZURE

The fourth amendment of the constitution provides citizens protection from unlawful search and seizure. Courts have consistently held that this amendment is aimed at police or persons acting on behalf of or in concert with police in effecting a search.

Security officers functioning in a shopping center environment are normally not acting with, or for, local police as they perform their duties. Additionally, security officers patrol on private property that has its own set of rules. Therefore, security officers acting on behalf of management on shopping center property have the right to conduct a reasonable search of a person or vehicle if circumstances dictate the necessity for a search.

An example of a reasonable search may involve the examination of the contents of a backpack carried by a patron onto shopping center property when the terror alert level is elevated. Clearly security officers should be encouraged to exercise restraint in any decision to effect a search. Officers should not become involved in a verbal altercation with patrons who refuse to submit to a reasonable search. In this instance patrons may be asked to leave the property for failure to comply with the security officer or with property rules.

Note: When interacting with loss prevention officers employed by tenants, mall security officers should avoid assisting in searches of persons suspected of shoplifting.

DETENTION, RESTRAINT, PHYSICAL FORCE

As officers perform their duties at a shopping center, plaza or community center they may be faced with highly emotional critical situations that demand an immediate decision. It is very important that the private security officer has a clear understanding regarding authority in effecting arrest, detention, restraint and use of force. Security officers must understand that while they may perform any of these acts, their power concerning these actions is far more limited than a police officer's. Because the act of arrest is so closely associated with detention and restraint, it is defined in this section:

Arrest may be defined as taking of a person into custody by authority of law for the purpose of charging him/her with a criminal offense.

Detention is the legally authorized holding in confinement of a person subject to court proceedings.

Restrain is to deprive of freedom or liberty.

Use of Force (only when officers must control a violent, assaultive or resisting individual) is the force that is reasonable and necessary to effectively bring an incident under control while protecting lives of others.

We see from simple definitions of arrest, detention and restraint and use of force that each action restricts freedom of movement and may be perceived as a custodial situation. Because of the finite or subtle difference in each of these actions, caution must be exercised by security officers in effecting any of them.

Courts throughout the country continually offer varying opinions and direction regarding detention, restraint and use of force. For purposes of this section, we will consider guidance provided by New York State law.

McKinney's New York Penal Law, Sections 35.25 and 35.30, suggests that a private citizen may use physical force upon another person in order to prevent larceny of or criminal mischief to property, or in order to effect an arrest or prevent an escape from custody. In Section 35.15 the law suggests that a private citizen may also use physical force upon another when and to the extent he reasonably believes it is necessary to defend himself or a third person from what he reasonably believes to be the use of unlawful physical force by such other person. It is under the same circumstances that a private security officer is authorized to use physical force in carrying out his duties.

In considering the legal guidelines of New York State (and many other states), private security officers are restricted in their actions to physically detain or restrain by using physical force unless he/she, or a third party, is physically threatened by another. A security officer may also restrain a person if, by virtue of his actions, that person is likely to bring harm to himself. If, however, that restraint includes the application of handcuffs or another restraining device and the restrained person perceives that by virtue of the restraint he/she is under arrest, the security officer and or his/her employee may be the subject of a claim for assault, false imprisonment or wrongful arrest.

Note: The use of handcuffs or other restraining devices should be limited to violent and/or assaultive situations where the perpetrator's actions clearly indicate that he/she is an imminent threat to the security officer or other parties in the immediate area. Security officers equipped with handcuffs should be trained by a certified instructor in the use of this restraining device and the proper situations to use them. Where possible, local police should be summoned for immediate assistance.

Rather than physically detaining parties who require security attention for their actions and are nonviolent, officers should be trained and instructed to verbally encourage these individuals to remain for the arrival of local police to resolve the matter. It is important that security officers understand, under most circumstances, that physical detention of any kind may be the functional equivalent of placing a person under arrest. With the limited authority of a private security officer, any such arrest or detention may result in a civil action.

LOSS PREVENTION VS. MALL SECURITY

Arguably no single area of mall security brings greater potential for civil litigation than security's interaction with mall shop tenants or anchor/department store loss prevention officers. While shoplifting is a serious security matter, it is primarily the retailer who must address this issue. It must be clearly explained and understood during the training process that security officers do not have the power of arrest or detention in this situation. Thus, when called upon by a tenant or loss prevention officer to *detain a shoplifting suspect,* officers must remember the extent of their authority. Again, unlawful detention for questioning or a search creates unnecessary exposure to civil action. Security officers must be trained to assist tenants in the identification of suspects and ask the suspect to remain for police. Suspects should never be searched by a security officer or at the direction of a security officer.

Security officers should be strictly trained and supervised *not to detain or search.* Officers should be schooled on how to encourage shoplifting suspects to await the arrival of the police department. Officers must understand that a citizen's arrest cannot be effected by anyone other than the person who observed the commission of the crime (shoplifting). Security officers should be trained not to engage in "hot pursuit" through the mall or garage, and they should not allow anyone else to give chase of a suspect. The safety of mall patrons is at stake. Tenants and loss prevention officers should be informed of security's function in order to preclude expectations that go beyond the provisions of the law.

STATE LEGISLATION

In recent years, a number of states have developed laws that license and regulate private security guards and investigative agencies. With the expanded use of private security in many different environments and situations, including augmentation of some public policing functions, many more states are developing private security legislation.

Additionally, the Private-Sector Liaison Committee of the International Association of Chiefs of Police has worked with a number of private security trade organizations to create and publish guidelines and recommendations regarding licensing, training and qualifications for private security officers.

In recent years, the image and value of private security has elevated itself such that private security is being used more and more to augment public police functions in traffic control, parking enforcement, crime scene preservation and many other areas.

The result of all of this attention brings a demand for higher levels of training and performance. Compliance agencies and procedures are being established to insure the quality of private security operations. The new focus on security officers, security providers and security operations is likely to enhance performance and effectiveness in years to come.

In the final analysis of the roles of the private security officer and the public police officer, we find that as much as their roles are similar, their operational performance is dissimilar by virtue of their authority level. Security officers patrolling in the shopping center environment are truly police officers without the same level of authority.

9 | Patrol Techniques and Procedures

Earlier in this text we discussed the importance of studying and understanding security requirements at a property. It was concluded that security needs are based on identified threats and vulnerabilities. For purposes of this chapter we will assume that after a proper study was concluded and the threats and vulnerabilities identified, it was determined that the shopping center, plaza or community center requires the services of a security officer presence. Consideration may be given to five (5) basic types of patrol or deployment techniques that may be suitable to a shopping center environment.

1. Fixed post
2. Foot patrol (moving)
3. Mobile patrol (vehicle, bicycle, open carts)
4. Covert patrol (surveillance—"stakeout")
5. Mounted patrol

Next, a number of factors may be considered prior to electing any one or more of the patrol or deployment techniques.

1. Number and location of points of ingress and egress from roadways
2. Size, type and configuration of parking facility
3. Contour of the parking surface
4. Configuration of the building
5. Number and location of entrances into and exits from the building
6. Patrol goals and objectives
7. Cost factors
8. Weather ranges
9. Lines of sight
10. Established customer and security trends

Patrol may be divided into two categories—foot patrol and vehicular patrol (including bicycles). Enclosed malls are likely to determine a need for interior and exterior patrol.

Exterior or perimeter patrol may be the single most important element in the security plan of a shopping center. Considering that the majority of all customers, merchants and employees typically come to shopping centers by automobile, the parking facility should be safe, secure and user-friendly. The exterior or perimeter security should be designed and operated in a manner to make customers feel safe, secure and comfortable while making potential criminals feel uncomfortable. While exterior patrol is commonly done in a vehicle or with a bicycle, foot patrol may be used on the exterior in certain instances. Highly visible and recognizable patrols trained to effectively move about the parking facility while observing any unusual activity serve a valuable purpose.

Interior security patrol is primarily a function of the security officer unit. Officers must be selected, trained and supervised in a professional manner in order to develop the kind of security officer required in a shopping center environment. As previously discussed, security officers are called upon to act as customer service representatives, tenant liaison people, safety officers and rules enforcers, to name a few areas of service. Because of their uniforms and presence, they will arguably be the most recognizable representative(s) of the property. For this reason, they must present themselves well in appearance and actions. Daily, management, tenants, customers, police and fire officials depend on their performance.

Understandably, neither foot patrol nor mobile patrol is exciting. In fact, constant observation of similar surroundings is likely to become boring. For this reason, it is suggested that, where possible, officers rotate assignments every two hours. This practice minimizes officer observation failures and stimulates the officer to a higher level of alertness in different surroundings. Unquestionably, officers must have total familiarity with the entire property in order to participate in patrol zone rotation.

Recognizing that all patrols are meant to deter and detect, officers should be trained to insure that they observe people and locations in their assigned area and insure that they are seen as they patrol. Officers should have an intimate knowledge of the entire property including an awareness of shortcuts and back alleys that may be used by perpetrators of criminal activity. All patrols should be random and "systematically unsystematic."

Whether on mobile patrol or foot patrol, officers should observe and report. The review and analysis of reported observations provide the foundation for future adjustments to staffing and deployment. Reported safety hazards and/or operational problems are reported to management and operations for prompt repair or correction (see Appendix B—Maintenance Checklist). Security officer observations should be noted on the individual officers' activity log (see Appendix B—Officer's

Daily Log). Incidents, safety hazards and operational problems should be the subject of separate reports (see Appendix B—General Incident Report).

Of the five (5) basic patrol techniques listed above, the covert or surveillance patrol technique is the least likely to be used in the shopping center environment. This technique is typically introduced when a property experiences a persistent criminal problem that has not been diminished as a result of an elevated level of visible security. In short, the perpetrators continue their actions despite reasonable efforts to deter. Prior to instituting covert patrols in an attempt to observe criminal activity, every effort should be made to enlist the assistance of local police to resolve a persistent crime problem. Any attempts at private covert patrol or a stakeout must be done with a clear understanding of the legal limitations and dangers of addressing a crime in progress.

Mounted patrol is typically used in situations where crowds are likely to gather. Patrol officers on mounts are very visible and prominent. Mounted patrol officers and their mounts must be highly trained and disciplined to effectively operate in the shopping center environment. Mounted patrols have been used effectively in parking lots at grand openings or during the busy holiday season. In addition to the deterrence value, the highly visible and approachable nature of the mounted patrol makes it a very effective public relations technique. Most private security guard companies do not offer this service. In fact, many public police departments have discontinued mounted patrols due to costs associated with a patrol technique that is not used consistently.

MOBILE PATROL

Mobile patrols are typically conducted in open parking lots and parking garages. The most effective and efficient patrol vehicle for a property depends largely on the size and configuration of the parking facility. Obviously, climate and expected weather conditions enter into any decision to use bicycles, mopeds or open carts. Regardless of the choice of patrol vehicle, it should be well marked, highly visible and easily recognized as a security vehicle. Vehicles and/or officer operators should be equipped with radio communication to a central station or other security officers.

Roof-mounted emergency bar lighting is commonly used in parking lot patrol. When activated, these lights serve notice of an active security patrol while at the same time providing an added degree of safety to officers patrolling parking areas. A number of security operations elect to activate the emergency lights at all times the patrol is active, while others use these lights intermittently. Those that consistently activate emergency bar lights feel that they gain greater deterrent value from the visibility of the lights. The intermittent users claim that by using the lights on an irregular basis, would-be perpetrators are unable to identify any routine. While it is difficult to determine which method of patrol is most effective, a number of customer surveys have determined that most shoppers claim to feel more comfortable when driving onto a property and observing a security vehicle patrolling with activated emergency lights.

In making a decision of whether or not to consistently activate emergency bar lighting, consideration should be given to two (2) factors:

1. Safety of the officer operator patrolling a parking lot
2. Random/unpredictable patrols aimed at avoiding tracking

In the event bicycles, mopeds or golf carts (open carts) are chosen as patrol vehicles, they too should be equipped with a pole-mounted emergency light or flag for recognition and safety.

Determining Factors In Vehicle Selection

Practicality—consider size and configuration of parking facility, open lot, long straightaways, mild or severe weather, etc.

Visibility—visibility from inside out (officer observation), easily recognizable to patrons

Maneuverability—requirement for frequent tight turns [in parking garage]

Cost—initial, operational — projected fuel, service and maintenance costs

Warranty—length, coverage

In recent years, property managers have elected to use everything from Sport Utility Vehicles (SUVs) to mopeds to various types of electrically and gas-operated open carts. While SUV's provide excellent visibility because of their size and height, they are not as maneuverable or cost-effective as a bicycle or moped. When considering bicycle, moped or open cart as a mobile patrol option, it is important to insure that these vehicles are sturdy and built to handle high usage. Additionally, officers operating bicycles and mopeds should be uniformed and equipped properly for their assignment. Site-specific factors dictate the type of vehicle most appropriate for your use.

Operating a patrol vehicle in a parking lot or garage is challenging at best. Asking a single security officer to observe and report as he negotiates a vehicle safely in and about large concentrations of parked and moving vehicles is a lot to require. For this reason it is important that mobile patrol officers are given training on how to effectively patrol as they drive. Whether in an intermediate-size vehicle or an open cart, officers should be instructed in defensive driving. It is not necessary that officers are constantly moving while on mobile patrol. Security officers are likely to observe more in a safer manner by periodically stopping their vehicle at selected points in the parking lot and using the stop as a time to observe what is occurring at and about that area of the lot. Stops should be random and, when possible, at a position that allows for maximum visibility (clear, open lines of sight).

It is an effective practice for mobile patrol officers who observe persons lingering near a vehicle or elsewhere in the parking area to ask, "Are you having car trouble?" or "May I be of assistance?" Depending on the response, this approach may be followed with a statement, "If you require assistance, I'll be patrolling in the area for the next several hours." Techniques such as these simple inquiries and comments are favorably accepted by legitimate customers and serve notice to would-be perpetrators that they are under observation.

Some security functions have equipped patrol vehicles with public address speakers to be used by security officers in communicating with persons in the parking areas. When used properly, this practice introduces an audio deterrence to the environment.

Clearly bicycles, mopeds and open carts are more economical to operate as patrol vehicles; however, they are not the practical year-round choice in many northern climates. For safety reasons these smaller, less noticeable vehicles should be operated with a high degree of care as they traverse parking lot and garages. Because they are extremely maneuverable, these mobile patrols make up for their lack of high profile by more frequent appearances within their assigned zones. Officers patrolling on bicycles, mopeds, open carts or other nontraditional means tend to attract attention and are thought of as being more approachable than officers in vehicles. This phenomenon is favorable in considering the use of nontraditional patrol vehicles. Bicycles can be used as part of an interior patrol after the close of normal business. Depending on the configuration of the building, the speed and ease of movement of the bicycle may provide broader coverage in less time.

As is the case with traditional vehicle patrol, it is important to provide special training to bicycle patrol officers. Bicycle patrol training will develop a safe, effective security application. In most situations bicycle patrols are used to augment traditional vehicle patrol in large parking facilities.

Consideration should be given to equipping security vehicles with the following items:

First aid kit	Auto accident report forms	Reflective vest
Flashlight	Incident report forms	Illuminating wand
Traffic cones	Flares	Mobile Patrol Logs
Post Orders	Parking Lot Lighting Report	
Tow Away Warning Notice		AED [if available]

It is a good practice to inspect any security patrol vehicle for safety and operability on a daily basis or at the commencement of each shift (see Appendix B—Simplified Daily Report -Motorized Security).

FOOT PATROL

In order to maintain the integrity of the overall security operation, it is important that the foot patrol officer demonstrate the same professional traits listed in the subchapter "Role of the Security Officer" in this book. In fact, because the foot patrol officer primarily conducting interior patrol is more likely to verbally interact with customers and tenants, it may be more important that he/she consistently exhibit noticeably high levels of honesty, courtesy, discipline and professionalism. Officer demeanor and appearance is of utmost importance as he conspicuously patrols his assigned zone or beat.

As in the instance of the mobile patrol officer, foot patrol officers should insure that patrol patterns are random and noticeable to all. Officers should be equipped with a two-way radio to effectively communicate with a central control location, management office and/or other officers.

Interior foot patrol zones identifying normal boundaries for each officer's primary area of responsibility can be established. These zones or beats may vary according to staffing levels during any given day of the week or time of day. Each beat or zone should have a set of post orders describing the primary boundaries of the patrol, specific items of note within that zone, and general guidelines in addressing known or anticipated situations. Post orders are guides for officers and should not be so specific that officers cannot use common sense and good judgment in performing their duties. Post orders should be written in simple language, indexed by subject, and each order should address only one subject. An example of a post order may be—" Trash Removal—Service Corridors." Within that post order, a security officer may find instructions on reporting unauthorized trash in a service corridor and how to deal with the responsible tenant. Post orders should be available to officers as they assume their assigned posts. Post orders for mobile patrols should remain in the patrol vehicle. A master set of post orders may be kept in a control location or in the management office.

Officers patrolling the common area of the mall can maximize their visibility by insuring that they pause at the busy areas of their patrol zone and at points of convergence. It is important that foot patrol officers identify a number of prominent points within their assigned zone that provide clear, open lines of sight while making themselves conspicuous.

Interior foot patrol officers should be encouraged to verbally interact with patrons, particularly greeting them as they enter the mall. This practice signals customers that they have been noticed and immediately establishes security recognition. This custom is also effective for plazas and community centers where foot patrol officers may be assigned to exterior sidewalks and commons areas or squares.

It is advisable for foot patrol officers to interact with merchants; however, they should be cautioned against lengthy conversation with any single tenant since it will interrupt his patrol responsibilities. Interacting with merchants familiarizes sales associates with security personnel and develops a sense of confidence and personal safety within the entire property. This practice is an effective and subtle proactive crime prevention technique.

Foot patrol officers should always walk with a purpose avoiding sluggish or lethargic strolling that clearly detracts from the professionalism of patrol.

FIXED POST SECURITY

A fixed post may be the most limited use of a security officer. In a traditional sense, fixed posts are used at points of entry to control access. In a shopping center setting, fixed posts may be designed to assist at a difficult traffic control point at or near a parking lot entrance. This application may be beneficial during extremely busy shopping seasons or days. Since the security officer's control of traffic onto or off of the property may impact vehicle traffic from or onto a public road, it may be advisable to coordinate this practice with the local police. Officers assigned to this type of fixed post provide an immediate high profile to customers entering the property. Some property managers have elected to station a security officer in or at a fixed security booth within the parking area of the center or plaza. In many instances, the booth is raised to provide added visibility about the area of the booth. There are security booths, huts or towers on the market that are mounted on wheels allowing for relocation of the tower from time to time. While the mobility of the observation booth allows for added flexibility, in the event of a parking lot incident, movement of the security location may open the door for a claim that the victim purposely parked in the area of the security post and at the time of the assault the post had been relocated. The use of fixed posts in parking lot and garages can be effective; however, since the security officer is stationary, it should be understood that officer exposure/visibility is limited.

ROOFTOP PATROL

In assigning security officers to rooftop patrol, management is relinquishing officer prominence for a useful and valuable point of observation. Rooftop patrol, while not totally fixed by nature, is limited and rarely seen by the average customer or merchant. This practice may be effective in detecting undesirable activity in an open parking lot; however, it is not cost-effective. Often times it may require the use of two officers working together to identify perpetrators because the rooftop patrol officer is unable to read a license number or observe subjects with enough detail to report to police for response. Even with the use of binoculars, the distance from rooftop to incident sight may be too far.

On very large properties, rooftop patrol officers are often used to detect traffic congestion. In this way one rooftop officer, with maximum observation, is able to direct the required number of mobile or foot patrol officers to strategic points assisting in traffic flow.

SPECIAL EVENT SECURITY

Since a "special event" is exactly as titled, it is logical to give consideration to a number of factors in developing a "special" security package tailored for the event. Most special events are developed and/or coordinated by the shopping center staff marketing director. It is important that the marketing director provide details concerning the event to the security director well in advance of the planned occurrence.

Together, the marketing director and security director can consider the following factors that may influence security staffing and deployment:

➢ Date and time of the event
➢ Period of time event will include
➢ Specific location, including boundaries, of the event
➢ Nature/type of event
➢ Expected attendance—numbers & type
➢ Anticipate media coverage
➢ Requirement for coordination with VIP security, local police
➢ Traffic consideration

Special events may vary from a large department store opening, to a parking lot carnival, to a seasonal feature event such as the arrival of Santa Claus. Where possible, security planning should be based on data or information derived from other similar events on the property. If the event is new to the property, it is advisable to do some pre-event research through a booking agent or by contacting other centers that may have hosted this feature. Pre-event investigation may provide valuable information regarding the size and type of crowd to expect. Obviously, all pre-event intelligence goes toward determining the level of staffing and type of deployment needed for a given event.

If it is determined that the event involves a VIP or celebrity who engages his/her own security, it will be necessary to coordinate security operations with them prior to the event. Since it can be expected that most special events will bring higher volumes of vehicle traffic to the center, potentially causing congestion on public roads leading onto and out of the parking lots, it is almost always a good idea to communicate with the local police. In providing the police advance notice, you will have satisfied necessary liaison and may augment your security operations at key points of ingress and egress.

Some of the security controls, measures and equipment that may be considered in special event planning are:

1. Enhanced communications—additional leased or rented radios
2. Independent special events command and communications
3. Traffic controls—separate special event parking
4. Pre-event printed informational, directional, safety and security guidelines
5. Special event public information & security booth location
6. Temporary barriers, brightly colored demarcation tape, traffic cones
7. Additional (temporary) lighting
8. Directional and informational signage
9. "Special Event" officer security vests—enhanced officer recognition
10. Megaphone—portable public address capability

The number and type of security controls, measures and equipment appropriate for a special event are dictated by the type of event, duration of the event and special event factors (previously listed) associated with the event. Advance security planning is meant to insure that there are adequate controls and measures in place to insure order and safety on and about the property.

DAILY LOGS AND INCIDENT REPORTS

A *Daily Activity Log* recording the name of each security officer, time on duty and post of assignment should be maintained at the Command and Communication Center. As officers are moved from post to post, or as they report "out of service" for the day, appropriate entries should be made. Any administrative notations (non-operational) may be recorded in this log. A sample entry may read—"8/12/04, 1400, SO 4 on duty post 3." If SO 4 is reassigned to post 2 later in the day, a log entry should be made indicating "1605, SO 4 assigned duty post 2."

A *Dispatcher's* or *Command and Communications Log* should be maintained by the dispatcher. This log should reflect all communications into and out of the Command and Communications Center. To facilitate locating specific log entries at a future date, entries should be number consecutively by year (for example, 0034—04 indicating log entry # 34 in the year 2004. Each entry should indicate the date, day of the week, time [military time] and nature of each communication). A complete example of a log entry may be—"0034–04, 8/19, Tu, 1307, report of lost child in food court." If an officer is dispatched to respond to a communication/log entry, the entry should reflect details of the dispatcher's communication with the officer. The next entry, numbered consecutively, should refer to the original communication and detail the dispatcher's communication (for example, 0035, 1308—SO 2 dispatched to food court in response to 0034–04, missing child in food court). To complete this sequence it is necessary that SO 2 communicate his findings to the dispatcher, which may be recorded as—"0036–04, 1316—SO 2 reports missing child item 0035–04 located at Delightful Donut kiosk east of the food court, child reunited with mother." All entries should reflect an opening and closing.

Activation of any alarms should appear on the log indicating the time and the nature of the alarm. Responses to the alarm should be included.

Individual *Security Officers Logs* should be maintained by each security officer to document his/her activity on each shift (see Appendix B). This log can be kept as simple as required by the Director of Security. These preprinted log sheets may include a series of numbered activity codes indicating typical officer duties or actions (for example, 23—checked roof hatch/locked—1725). The use of pre-assigned activity codes simplifies recording for officers as they conduct patrols. Activity codes are a good way of tracking and documenting security officer performance and activity.

It is advisable to maintain Daily Activity Logs and Dispatcher Logs for a minimum of three years. All logs, incident reports, videos, time cards, schedules or other business records generated in the routine course of business should be cataloged and preserved as they relate to a critical incident on the property. These will be a part of a *Potential Litigation File* (discussed in the chapter "The Reality of Security and the Law"). Such documentation may serve to assist in defending against a costly lawsuit.

INCIDENT REPORTS

Incident Reports clearly describing *who, what, when, and where* should be prepared by security officers for every incident he/she addresses. Blank incident reports should be developed by the Security Director to assist security officers in reporting all necessary information. Incident report forms should be carried by security officers as they conduct patrols. When officers are faced with an incident, report forms will prompt them to obtain and record pertinent information. *A sample Incident Report appears in the appendix of this book.*

COMPUTERIZED INCIDENT REPORTING AND TRACKING SYSTEM

There are currently a number of information technology companies that specialize in the development of software programs designed to assist in incident tracking and case management. Based on information derived from incident reports, these programs may track incidents by category and frequency by day of the week, hour of the day, and location on the property. A number of contract security officer companies use information management software as an integral part of their operation. Incident reporting and tracking (applicable to large properties) helps management to constantly review and evaluate security operations at the center. Security information management programs are very useful in cost-based activity tracking. The security officer function can be effectively and efficiently staffed, deployed, and managed based on information reported and analyzed through an information management system.

No matter what patrol procedure or technique is employed, with the exception of the covert patrol or surveillance, the primary purpose of any patrol is to observe, report, and deter. Unless the patrol technique appropriate for the post is utilized, security officers will be unable to successfully accomplish their intended objectives and may become ineffective. In reaching a determination regarding the proper patrol technique for a given post, it should be kept in mind that the security officer functioning in the shopping center environment should be able to carry out the additional customer service, property and assets protection, and rules enforcement duties that give him/her added value as part of the mall team.

10 | Security Equipment, Measures and Controls

In response to society's increased interest and concern for better security, modern electronic and computer technology companies have swiftly and positively impacted the security hardware and software market. More efficient and sophisticated products are being developed and produced so rapidly that recently purchased equipment is perceived as being obsolete long before expectations. New security products operate faster, are stronger, have greater capabilities and often record their performance in real time and historically. There are smart cards, biometric access controls, multiplexers, graphic user interfaces and integrated locking systems. There are advanced guard tour monitoring systems and multiple site management CCTV systems. Things that, in the past, may have been thought of as science fiction visions are real and in use today in many environments. Because all of this new technology is available does not necessarily mean that it must or should become a part of your property's security operation. Clearly many of these new hi-tech security products are highly effective and may be a perfect fit for a large number of end users, but sometimes simpler equipment, measures and controls may be better.

As was suggested in the risk analysis and threat assessment of our *Step One* approach (Chapter 3), it is prudent and advisable to analyze the total security requirements for your property prior to the purchase of expensive security equipment, controls and/or measures. No single component of a safety and security plan should stand alone. In that regard, any decision to purchase and implement security hardware and/or software should be done with a vision of how the new measure or control will integrate with the planned or existing security function.

In determining the requirement for security hardware, software or a physical security presence, it is important to understand the proper application of each item or product and how it will integrate into the overall plan. It is with this approach in mind that we will discuss a number of security equipment, measures and controls.

There is no intention to suggest that any or all of the security contols or measures discussed in this text are required components of a reasonable and adequate security plan. As has been emphasized previously, each property must be considered independently in order to conclude what measures, controls and procedures are best suited to the overall security plan.

The following is a list a number of security controls and measures often used in the shopping center environment along with common applications for each of them. Since many of the items listed may be driven or triggered by a number of different technologies, and since the capabilities of each technology are ever-changing, it is impractical to discuss each of them and their qualities in detail. Once it is decided that a specific measure or control is appropriate and for your property, it is then that you should discuss the most effective and efficient technology associated with that control with a qualified independent security consultant.

SIGNAGE

Operating under the assumption that each customer entering the property is coming there for the first time, attractive, well-positioned signs are helpful in directing motorists and pedestrians to their desired destination quickly and in an orderly manner. Signs at or near parking lot or garage entrances and exits help to maintain an even flow of traffic at critical points of convergence. Informational signs may be located within the property lots or garages indicating speed limits, pedestrian crossings or parking location (pole markers). Property orientation signage (wayfinding systems) minimizes the number of customers who may wander about the center or parking lot looking for their vehicle. Patrons drifting aimlessly through parking lots are likely to become targets for criminal assault.

Safety and security tips such as *Remember to lock your vehicle* or *Lock all packages in your trunk* may be posted about the lot as customer security reminders. This, and similar customer-friendly signage is useful and appreciated by customers and becomes a value-added feature to your center's business and security atmosphere. Signs indicating the location of life safety devices such as AEDs (defibrillators) are helpful.

Property rules may be displayed prominently at selected locations about the property to reinforce management's message of structure and order at the center. Though not commonly thought of as a component of a security package, attractive signage, when used in conjunction with complementary measures and controls, becomes an economical, practical and effective asset to your overall security plan.

LIGHTING—PARKING LOT & GARAGES

Possibly the single most important business and security feature of a shopping center, plaza or community center is the parking facility. Upwards of an estimated 70% (seventy percent) of all customers, employees, and visitors will come to centers by car; therefore, the parking facility must be safe, secure, and user-friendly. Mall patrons should *perceive* and experience a feeling comfort in the parking facility and potential criminals must feel uncomfortable. Much of the success of any center weighs on the shoppers' willingness to return to the parking facility.

A lighting system should be installed throughout parking garages and decks that provides adequate illumination for customer visibility and easy detection of criminal behavior. Fixtures should be positioned to provide an even level of lighting for the entire parking surface. Consideration may be given to enhanced lighting treatment at areas of convergence such as stairwells, entrances and walkways.

As you develop or evaluate your property lighting package, it is advisable to reference publications developed and distributed by the Illuminating Engineering Society of North America (IESNA). IESNA is recognized as the preeminent authority in the United States on lighting standards and recommendations. IESNA publications provide very specific lighting recommendations for a broad range of environments. Other lighting references are available.

FENCING AND BARRIERS

In considering the use of barriers or fencing at your property, it should be clearly understood that virtually all natural or man-made barriers or fencing may be compromised or defeated. For purposes of an open environment such as a shopping center, plaza or community center, perimeter fencing, in most instances, defines property boundaries and directs vehicle and foot traffic to authorized entrances and exits. Walls or fencing erected at the perimeter of isolated parking areas may serve as deterrents to the less determined or motivated individual but should not be considered as a preventive measure.

Consideration may be given to fencing critical areas such as electrical generators, air handling units, liquid fuel containers and retention ponds within the property boundaries. While fencing or barriers may be a proper application for such locations, it should be kept in mind that this measure is a deterrent that may need to be integrated with other security features (lighting, patrol, alarms). When constructing fencing or barriers, care should be taken not to create areas of cover and concealment.

The use of permanent and moveable bollards, particularly at mall entrances, has become a common barrier application. These installations are meant to prevent "smash and grabs" as well as suicide bomber vehicle entrance. In considering the use of bollards, composition and spacing of the posts are very important. Large decorative planters made of cast iron or concrete may serve as a reasonable alternative to bollards at entrances.

LOCKS AND LOCKING DEVICES

The diverse nature, kinds of activities, and public access aspect of the shopping center environment bring a number of factors to mind when considering locking requirements at a given center. Considerations may include but may not be limited to:

➢ Standard hours of operation
➢ Building or property configuration
➢ After-hours entertainment venues
➢ Building and fire codes
➢ Tenant security
➢ Loading dock provisions
➢ Common access areas—exclusive access areas

It is a good rule of thumb to develop a locking plan that secures as much of the common area as practical when the mall is closed. If late-night restaurant or entertainment tenants do not have separate exterior entrances, it is suggested that a partial lockdown plan be developed to secure those portions of the property that are not being used. Exterior doors that are not considered emergency exits should be locked after normal mall hours. A complete lockdown of the property, where possible, may reduce the requirement for the number of officers patrolling during the late evening and early morning hours.

Every property has different locking requirements based, in part, on the above-listed factors. In order to maintain the integrity of your key control protocol, whatever your locking system may be, it is important to develop a workable key management and control plan. It is through this associated plan that property management can minimize access to exclusive access areas of the property.

ALARMS AND ALARM SENSORS

Typically, in a public-access facility such as a shopping center, plaza or community center, local fire and building codes dictate the installation of fire and/or smoke alarms. The requirement for these mandated alarms originates with public safety concerns. Codes may also require that fire suppression systems such as sprinkler systems are alarmed to assure their operational effectiveness. Elevator malfunction alarms are also commonly required by local code.

Unlike the code-mandated alarms, installation of alarms associated with intrusion is generally the decision of property management. Large super-regional shopping centers with many emergency exit doors find it suitable to electronically alarm these doors, making it easier to monitor unauthorized entry or door propping. Alarms associated with emergency exits may be configured to annunciate at the point of entry or at a common annunciator panel in a security control room.

Motion sensors associated with alarms or cameras may be used in service corridors. This type of installation is normally not activated until after the close of business since service corridors are active with merchants and vendors during business hours.

There are any number of sensor technologies on the market that will trigger when there is intrusion at point of alarm, elevated temperature, presence of smoke, decrease in water pressure, loss of electricity or tampering with the sensory device. The proper application of an alarm sensor device and the correct alarm is a decision to be made by the property owner or manager based on determined security needs. With the exception of code-mandated alarms, the decision to include alarms in your security plan must be determined case-by-case after complete analysis.

Note: It is advisable to enlist the assistance of a staff security professional or an independent security consultant to determine alarm needs, applications and appropriate technology for your center.

Local codes commonly require that smoke and/or fire alarms annunciate at a fire station or emergency control center. Burglar or intrusion alarms may also be connected to a police department alarm panel or a central monitoring location. Because activation of these alarms requires an active response, alarm vendors and installers should be required to provide assurances against a specific number of false alarms. Police and fire companies in many municipalities charge a fee when they respond to false alarms beyond a specific number. Sometimes it is possible to reach an agreement with the responding agency for the local security function to verify the authenticity of an alarm prior to dispatching a unit. This authority carries with it the benefit of neutralizing and resetting the alarm.

Since all alarms require a physical response, they must be managed effectively by designated staff personnel or a private central monitoring location.

EMERGENCY/CUSTOMER ASSISTANCE CALL BOXES

Consideration may be given for the inclusion of emergency call boxes or customer assistance telephone or intercom systems in parking lots and/or garages. These remote phone systems commonly communicate directly with a control center and are designed to provide immediate and direct voice communication for persons in need of assistance. Call boxes may be mounted on light poles, building supports, columns, walls or as freestanding stations. These devices normally have a recognizable light or strobe affixed to them. They are usually signed for "emergency" or "customer assistance" on all visible sides.

If it is decided to include emergency or customer assistance call boxes in your security plan, consideration for installation should be given to stairwells, stairwell entrances, areas of convergence and isolated or remote areas of parking lots or garages.

If a closed circuit camera system is in place or if one is projected, consideration may be given to integrating the camera system into the call box function such that a camera would focus on the call station when the call for aid is activated. It is advisable to regularly test call boxes or any emergency system to avoid system failure at a critical time. Necessary repairs should be made promptly.

PREPROGRAMMED PAY TELEPHONES—EMERGENCY CALLING

Through an arrangement with the pay telephone vendor servicing your center, it is possible to have all public telephones on the property programmed to a specific code (for example, 411) that creates an immediate no-cost connection to the security control center of any predetermined location on the property. When telephones are programmed in this manner, each instrument should be signed "Dial 411 for Security Assistance." This measure, in effect, establishes each of the pay telephones located throughout the property as an emergency call station.

CLOSED CIRCUIT TELEVISION—CCTV

When considering a closed circuit television (CCTV) system at your property, do not consider it as a replacement for physical security presence. Rather, CCTV is an augmentation of a security officer function. Cameras and video monitors are designed to capture activity in areas where it is impossible or impractical to provide a continuous presence. Once the activity has been observed by a camera, it may require a physical response. While cameras and associated monitoring and recording devices have the ability of observing and recording events, cameras are not capable of preventing or responding to the event. It is not a good practice to install a camera system with recording equipment with no intention of monitoring the system; also, it is not a good practice to display "dummy" cameras. Courts have found that the presence of cameras that are not working or that are not being monitored provide a false sense of security to third parties. Therefore, in reaching a decision of whether or not to include CCTV in your security plan, it is prudent to incorporate a monitoring station, a person to monitor the system, and a minimum of one officer to respond to events as they are captured.

CCTV systems may be integrated with intrusion alarms, emergency call boxes, and access control devices. Fixed and moveable (pan, tilt and zoom) cameras may be used to monitor and/or record activity in or about the exterior of the property. The following is a list of some of the common uses or applications for camera coverage:

➤ Parking lots and garages
➤ Common area (interior)
➤ Entrance/exit corridors
➤ Elevators and escalators
➤ Areas outside of rest rooms
➤ Food court
➤ Loading docks

Where CCTV systems are in place, or if a camera system is planned for a property, it is a good practice to have security officers communicate with the security control center requesting camera coverage of any incident addressed by an officer. This procedure generates photographic evidence of security officer performance and may minimize claims of excessive force or improper officer behavior.

In the event a critical incident occurs on your property and that incident is captured and recorded on the CCTV recording equipment, it is a good idea to make a copy of the incident recording prior to turning photographic evidence over to the police. Oftentimes videotapes or digital recordings that become a part of a criminal proceeding become misplaced within the system and are no longer available in the event of a civil action against the owner/manager.

To be sure, there is much to be considered in selecting the components of a CCTV system that best suit your needs. Cameras, lenses, signal transmission cables, monitoring or head-end equipment, control apparatus and recording equipment should be properly coordinated to assure that the camera system performs at peak efficiency and is appropriate for its intended use (environment).

Note: In view of the expense and complexity of a CCTV system involving multiple cameras, it is highly advisable to retain an independent consultant to develop specifications for the proposed system and each of its components.

When contracting with a camera vendor, it is advisable to include a service contract. Contract language should provide for prompt response, (as close to twenty-four [24] hours as possible) to requests for camera or system repair.

GUARD TOUR SYSTEM

The guard tour system is an electronic administrative tool that assists in tracking security officer performance. Unlike the old security watchman's clock system that tracked officer rounds by recording the time he/she inserted a key into receivers at predetermined stations along a designated patrol route, today's technology allows a security officer to swipe a wand or insert a small hand-held electronic instrument into a receiver affixed to a stationary object. The guard tour system has the capability of recording the time of the officer's appearance, observations at that station (mechanical door found open or locked, etc.), and any stations missed on the officer's patrol route. Information gathered from the guard tour may be downloaded into reports and exceptions noted by the officer can be addressed as necessary. While guard tour systems may be integrated into daily daylight patrols, they are typically used during the evening or non-business hours.

KEY CONTROL SYSTEMS

Shopping centers, plazas, and community centers may be described as compartmentalized when considering all of the separate areas that coexist at one property. In addition to tenant spaces, there are loading docks, storage areas, electrical rooms, mechanical rooms, building management control rooms, administrative offices, and security control space, to name a few. Everyone on the property does not have access to all of these spaces. For this reason, key control and management is a necessity and can become problematic if it does not receive adequate attention. A number of key and lock companies and security equipment vendors have developed electronic key control systems to assist in key control and management. These systems range from the simple to very sophisticated and use a broad range of technologies to function. In considering the possible implementation of a key control system, it should be understood that none of these systems are totally problem-free and each requires some level of human involvement. Key control systems, if operated diligently, do enhance the capability to identify and trace lost or missing keys.

RADIO COMMUNICATIONS

Communication is at the very heart and soul of shopping center operations. Because of the size, configuration, diversity of activities, and number of tenants and customers, it is essential that management and security communicate with staff operations, tenants, and community services including police, fire and emergency services. If the property includes a security officer function, officers can operate more effectively and efficiently with a reliable two-way radio system. Messages related to safety, security, traffic control, tenant requests and many more can be delivered promptly for the required response or action. If officers do not have direct communication with the local police, fire, and emergency response departments, they should have a radio contact point that can forward messages or requests to them (security control station or management office).

Note: Some security functions provide the security shift supervisor with a cell phone as a secondary means of communication to be used as required.

SECURITY OFFICER UNIFORMS AND EQUIPMENT

Uniforms and Appearance

Since security officers are likely to be the most easily recognizable and identifiable members of the shopping center staff, it is important that, through their appearance, they create a good impression on customers. The impression customers and visitors get when they observe security officers *(perception)* will, in all probability, carry over to the entire management organization. A neat professional appearance brings about respect and deference to the position. Personal cleanliness and grooming are highly important in creating a favorable first impression.

Most security officer staffs pattern their appearance after municipal or state police. In keeping with that theme, many private security functions favor a long-sleeved white or light-colored shirt with a tie. White is frequently used because it is noticeable and delivers a message of aid or assistance. The long-sleeved shirt with a contrasting dark tie delivers a message of formality and authority. Because security officers may frequently be in and out of a vehicle, at loading docks, or patrolling service corridors, it is advisable to provide them with dark trousers to minimize the appearance of stains and dirt seen more easily on light-colored trousers. A black belt and shined black shoes serve to complement the officer's overall appearance.

Officers' shirts should prominently display a patch, insignia, or badge identifying them as a security officer for the property. It is appropriate and effective to have some insignia that associates the officer with the mall displayed on the shirt. In states where security officer certification or licensing is required to be displayed on the person, this should be worn in accordance with regulations.

To insure that officers appear daily with properly laundered uniforms, they should be issued three (3) uniform shirts and two (2) pair of trousers. Included in the initial uniform issue (depending on climate) should be one (1) commando-type sweater, one (1) cold weather jacket or parka, and one (1) clear or bright-colored rain jacket.

Officer visibility and recognition is often enhanced with high-profile hats. The eight-point patrol hat and the sheriff's or "Smokey the Bear" hat seem to be the most effective. Although the least expensive, the security baseball-style cap detracts from the professional appearance that a highly effective security function strives to achieve.

Displaying security officer rank with collar and/or sleeve insignia on the security officer uniforms can create noticeable organizational structure. In most situations, security officers tend to respond favorably to this display of rank and perform at higher levels as they strive to achieve the next rank.

Bicycle Patrol Uniforms

Because bicycles are used primarily outdoors in a parking lot or garage setting, it is necessary to uniform bike patrol officers with garments that are designed specifically for bicycle riding. Bike patrol officer uniforms should be brightly colored and/or reflective for officer safety. Uniforms should prominently display a badge, insignia or words that make them clearly recognizable as security officers. Bicycle patrol officers should be equipped with helmets that may also indicate security.

Officer Equipment

In addition to the officer uniform issue described above, a standard security officer equipment issue may include, but may not be limited to:

1. duty belt with key holder
2. streamline tactical flashlight with belt holder
3. whistle
4. two-way radio with remote microphone/speaker (radio holster)
5. notepad and pen
6. duty log or activity report form
7. incident report forms
8. blood-borne pathogen or infectous disease control kit

Depending on the philosophy of management and/or the contract security officer company, officers may be equipped with restraining devices such as handcuffs or flex cuffs. Officers may also be equipped with a baton or a chemical spray dispenser. If officers are so equipped, they should be properly trained in the use of this equipment and certified as required by state or local laws.

Prior to issuing handcuffs, flex cuffs or any other restraining device, it is advisable to establish a written policy that clearly defines when a personal restraining device may be used. Unless security officers have been deputized as peace officers or special police, they should not apply handcuffs unless, in the officer's judgment, a person is a threat to him- or herself, others in the immediate area, or the officer. A similar policy should be established as it relates to the use of a tactical baton, chemical spray or any other personal defense weapons issued to officers. Records of training and certifications related to personal defense weapons and restraining devices should be maintained in the security officer's personnel file.

Other security officer equipment considerations may be body armor, gas mask, megaphone (portable public address system), basic first aid kit, and portable flashing safety lights. As mentioned in "Radio Communications" previously, a number of larger security functions provide shift supervisors with cell phones to be used as backup communication.

While it is not necessary that every shopping center, plaza, or community center have each of the discussed security measures, controls, or equipment, the installation and effective use of some of the basic controls and measures such as signage, lighting and fencing or barriers will serve to establish higher levels of order at any given property. Clearly, factors such as building configuration, size, location, tenant mix and demographics may influence the number and type of security measures and controls included in your security operation.

11 | Guidance and Direction for Security Operations: The Security Manual

We've all heard reference to the ship without a rudder when people discern that a task is not being performed in an orderly fashion. We know that an automobile manufacturer would not design and develop a car with sleek, attractive lines, a high-performance engine, computerized instrumentation and controls, and an on-board navigation system without equipping the vehicle with a steering wheel. Likewise, we cannot design and develop a security function without providing guidance and direction to those who will implement the various components of that function on a daily basis.

Whether you have a very simple security plan at a small shopping plaza or a more complex security operation at a large super-regional mall, the function is likely to have a number of components that will require some level of staff performance to make them work effectively. The plaza's security package may consist of parking lot lighting, signage and tenant/management communications, while the super-regional mall's security function may include CCTV, various alarm systems and a security officer operation. Even though the much smaller plaza property has fewer components to its security package, it necessitates human involvement to insure that lighting is repaired and replaced on a timely basis, that signage is updated and properly placed, and that tenants and management communicate critical information to each other. Experience tells us that whenever there is a human element involved in a mechanical or procedural function, it is prudent to provide an instructional manual, thus, the security manual.

It has been emphasized repeatedly throughout this text that security requirements and plans should be tailored to the individual property. The same proposition holds true for the development of rules and actions published in a security manual. Clearly, the policies and procedures established for use at a plaza are likely to be far different from those created for a super-regional mall. It is, however, important, in each instance, to craft guidelines that give direction to your security function.

From a liability standpoint, failure to develop a security manual may be interpreted by the courts as a significant breakdown in a property manager's efforts to provide reasonable and adequate security procedures for the protection of customers and employees. The old belief that "if we don't put it in writing, we can't/won't be held responsible" will no longer stand. The existence of a security manual demonstrates that a property manager is proactive in the security function and has policies and procedures in place to address that which is reasonably foreseeable.

With the proper training and supervision, a security manual will provide employees the kind of guidance and direction necessary to carry out his or her security responsibilities in an effective and efficient manner. The security manual may be used as a training tool for new hires and a ready reference for daily activities. If the security manual includes an emergency management section, the manual may be used as a reference in emergency situations.

What follows is a reprint of *A Guide to Writing a Shopping Center Security Manual* that was published by the International Council of Shopping Centers in 2003. This guide was published for study and informational purposes. The guidelines set out in this publication are not absolute and should be tailored to your specific property.

WHO SHOULD BE INVOLVED

Although the center manager may be in charge of the project, the actual "legwork" will probably be done by either the security director or the operations director, or by the two working together. However, in order to have a fully comprehensive manual, you will probably want to involve all the departments of center management, each of which will bring a different point of view to the book.

The marketing director will get involved because of security's public relations role during disasters or emergencies and special events, which relates to the center's overall image with customers. Marketing should also be consulted because security officers interact daily with tenants and customers, and tenant/center relationships are also part of the marketing function.

Engineering people should help write the procedures so that, for example, there is no chance that an uninformed security guard will turn on a panel of lights during a patrol in such a way that an energy peak occurs that damages other aspects of the center's operations.

Personnel people can help with sections on job descriptions, selection, both initial and ongoing training, and behavior and dress codes.

The completed manual should then be sent to corporate headquarters where, depending on the organization's structure, it should then be reviewed by any or all of the following departments:

1. Risk Management
2. Operations/Management
3. Legal
4. Security
5. Regional Management

You will probably also want to have your center's local legal counsel review the entire book, paying particular attention to the areas of weapons, arrests and uniforms. *It is absolutely crucial that all the security policies and procedures in the manual conform to the statutes and ordinances that govern your center's activities and that govern behavior in your locality.*

Some suggest adding to your manual a requirement which states that "The local security director is responsible for maintaining copies of all state and local laws, ordinances and/or regulations pertinent to the center's security program." Or you may want to consider actually quoting local laws in the manual. However, if you do this, the laws must be made absolutely clear, which will probably require the aid of a lawyer who represents the center. Any change or modification to these laws must be reflected in the security manual.

WRITING A SECURITY MANUAL

PROGRAM OBJECTIVES

Most security manuals begin with a statement of the purpose of the security department. Example: "The purpose of the Safety and Security Department is to provide a safe and secure place for employees and shoppers alike. Enforcement of laws pertaining to the property's operations is a responsibility of this department."

A statement of purpose might be worded this way: "The manager must ensure that the security program at the center is properly and professionally carried out in order to create a safe and secure environment for invitees and tenant employees, to deter crimes against persons or property, and to contribute to public and community relations."

The authority of the security personnel is derived from their status as "a citizen" as well as from a private property owner's rights and responsibilities in carrying out the policies of the owner and the protection of the owner's property. Security personnel typically have no police authority unless an individual security officer has been commissioned by the state to bestow limited "police powers." Because

---

Format of Your Manual

Before you write a security manual, you might want to think about how it will be used and distributed. These are some questions you might want to ask:

1. Who will read the manual? All center personnel? Security director? New security people? Tenants?
2. Will the manual be distributed or will it stay in one office?
3. Do you want a loose-leaf or clipped-together format to facilitate changes?
4. Do you want the information in one book or in several small booklets (perhaps divided into topics such as, "Shopping Center Security," "Customer/Tenant Assistance," "Reports," "Emergency Procedures," and "Disaster Plan Guidelines")?
5. How will you index the manual for maximum efficiency?

---

these rights can differ from state to state and city to city, it is incumbent on the local staff to have an understanding of the latitude they have in controlling behavior on their property.

CENTER RULES AND POLICIES

In this section, the security manual may list center policies that govern the behavior of customers. These policies, or rules, may be posted somewhere in the center and may appear in a tenant's manual although not all shopping centers have a "code of conduct" specified in their manuals. Since the security officers will most often be the people enforcing these rules, it is a good idea to spell them out in the security manual, if policies concerning behavior exist. Some centers print rules and policies on a small card, which security officers can distribute to customers.

The security manual lists center policies that govern the behavior of customers. These policies, or rules, may be posted somewhere in the center and may also appear in a tenant's manual.

There are several ways to bring the rules to the attention of security manual readers. For example:

1. List the policies *without* elaborating on security's role in enforcing them
2. List the policies and *indicate* security's role in enforcing each one.

One expert suggests that the manual may precede the listing of policies with this general advice: "Serious security problems must be handled quickly and properly, but good public relations has to be incorporated at all times when dealing with the public. A combination of common sense, professionalism and training will enable the security officer to handle all situations in a safe and courteous manner."

However, one manual may later detail an eight-step procedure for dealing with trespassers, from 1. Stop the individual and identify yourself as center security, through 7. Upon arrival of the police (who are called only when other means of encouraging the trespassers to leave have failed), inform them of the violation(s) and allow them to do their function. 8. The time and date of the notification of trespassing must be documented.

Among the center policies to be listed are those dealing with:

1. Proper attire
2. Alcohol and other controlled substances
3. Weapons
4. Conduct, which includes loitering. (It may be helpful to provide specific statements of policy, such as, *"Loitering Groups:* Individuals or groups shall not be allowed to loiter or congregate in any portion of the shopping center. Security officers should give special attention to any locations where this condition exists.")
5. Noise
6. Bikes/Skates/Skateboards
7. Animals
8. Parking lot regulations
   a. Handicapped parking
   b. Fire lanes
   c. Speeding

Differences Between Corporate and Local Manuals

A corporate security manual contains corporate policy and philosophy on such items as firearms, dealing with the press, giving first aid assistance, helping motorists and many other items. It describes the preferred procedures for carrying out the policies. It may be looked on as similar to an outline.

A local security manual fills in what may have been left out of the outline, which are items that relate to:

1. Local laws and ordinances
2. Policies of local fire, police and other departments
3. The size and layout of the physical property
4. The tenant mix
5. The customer mix.

However, all corporations review local manuals to ensure that the procedures described in the local manuals will conform to the procedures outlined in the corporate manual.

---

9. Vehicles
   a. Abandoned vehicles
   b. Overnight parking
10. Solicitation and advertising
11. Trespassing
12. Panhandling.
13. Youth access restrictions (if any)

SECURITY POLICY

Job Description

Although the security manual is itself a type of "job description" for the center's security department, you might want to add to the manual, probably quite near the beginning, a general statement about the role of the security officer. Among the responsibilities you might mention are providing a comfortable shopping atmosphere for customers and tenants alike.

Another part of the general job description might include how the security department fulfills its responsibilities, such as:

1. Foot and vehicle patrols
2. Responding to alarms and calls for help
3. Interacting with center management and retailers
4. Interacting with individuals and community agencies such as police and fire departments and the press
5. Training the shopping center community to cope with emergencies

---

Differences Between Policy and Procedure

A "policy" tells *what* and may often discuss *why* something is to be done, while a "procedure" describes *how* it is to be done. Policy is similar to philosophy while procedures deal with implementation.

An example of a policy is the statement that "The security officer is not a law enforcement officer. Security officers have no more powers of arrest than the average citizen."

A policy pertaining to emergencies might be expressed by saying that the center manager's main concerns in any emergency shall be:

1. The safety of center patrons, employees and the center itself
2. The protection of property
3. The security and preservation of company documents
4. An accurate reporting of the details pertaining to the emergency

---

One way to summarize the responsibilities of the security officer is to state that his main responsibility is the preservation of order throughout all public areas in the shopping center.

The security manual could state that the shopping center's security department is charged with the protection of all physical property and the enforcement of all rules and regulations set forth by management.

Responsibilities you might mention in a security manual are:
1. *Securing the safety of customers and retailers' employees*
2. *Securing the developer's property against loss*
3. *Assisting both customers and retailers*

In a section on "Disaster Plan Guidelines," one mall manager suggests that a summary of the department's purpose to establish a formal plan of action to minimize the danger to life, health and property from emergencies or disasters, and to take necessary and prudent steps to assure continuity of operations and restoration of normal business activities, be included.

As part of a general description of security work at your center, you might include an *organization* chart covering all center personnel, as well as specific instructions on the chain of command. Chain of command within the center management must be preserved in order to maintain principles and sound administration. It is highly important to the successful management of a center that the security/safety director and the maintenance supervisor work together in a spirit of mutual cooperation.

Hiring and Qualifications
Depending on the audience for your manual, you may or may not wish to include a broadly worded section on qualifications for being hired by your security department.

A general statement under a section entitled "Standards, Selection and Hiring Policy" could say that "The center manager shall be responsible for the selection and hiring of security officers. Care shall be taken to select individuals who have the intelligence, judgment and discretion to perform effectively." You might also want to add that "The center manager will not discriminate against any employee or applicant for employment because of race, color, religion, sex, national origin or age." This kind of sentence should be reviewed by local counsel because discrimination laws can vary for different communities.

One developer suggests that more detail could be included as "Desirable Traits for Security Officers" under these broad headings:

- Responsibility, honesty and conscientiousness
- Reading and writing communicative skills
- Leadership skills—exercising responsible authority over people and property
- Ability to make critical and acute observations
- Satisfactory background (i.e., having nothing in background that would interfere with effectiveness as a security officer).

Training

This section might begin with a general policy statement concerning the importance of training in the work of a security officer. It might also tell readers:

1. All training will conform with local statutes and laws
2. All training will be given by a qualified security trainer
3. All training will be documented as to:
   a. Who received it
   b. When it was completed
   c. Who administered it
   d. Topics covered
   e. Description of method (i.e., class discussion, demonstration, etc.)
4. All outside security personnel—usually hired on a temporary basis—will receive the same training as permanent staff members
5. Provisions for continuing, ongoing, systematic training of people already on the job
6. Description of criteria used to determine whether person has been trained adequately to meet hiring and retention standards.

You may then want to include a list of the broad general topics in which security personnel will be trained. The following topics might be among those you cover:

1. Alarm response procedures (smoke, fire, water flow, etc.)
2. Bomb threat and terrorist threat procedures
3. Cooperation with local law enforcement agencies and monitoring Homeland Security advisories
4. Courtesy and customer assistance
5. Effective communication
6. Emergency procedures
7. Fire prevention. (Center managers shall make every effort to have the security officers trained by the local fire department in the proper and safe use of fire extinguishers.)
8. Lost or missing child procedures

9. Proper patrol procedures
10. Report writing
11. Safe and defensive driving techniques
12. Safety and loss prevention
13. Traffic control

Uniforms and Grooming

You may be regulated by local laws regarding what type of uniform is permitted for nongovernment security guards. Be sure to check with legal counsel and corporate headquarters before making final policy with regard to uniforms. It may also be beneficial to contact local law enforcement officials regarding choice of uniforms (for example, similar or different colors, badge type, etc.).

Some topics you might want to include are:

- Issuance, ownership, care and surrender of uniforms
- Where uniforms can be worn
- Components of uniform—shirts, pants, skirts, jackets, hats, badges—and summer and winter variations
- Proper display of insignia, badges, hats, etc.
- Where and when hat is to be worn
- Importance of "spit and polish" appearance (i.e., shirts buttoned, shoes shined, insignia gleaming, proper fit of all clothing)

The manual might also deal with all personal aspects of appearance other than uniforms. Among the items to be discussed are:

- Hair: length and condition
- Beards and moustaches
- Jewelry
- The carrying of bundles, packages, umbrellas or other articles while in uniform. Example: Prohibited except where necessary in the performance of security duties.

Conduct/Behavior

Most center managers agree that security officers on duty are to conduct themselves in a special way that both makes them models of behavior and leaves them alert to anything unusual that may be happening in the center. Among the areas of behavior to be noted are:

- Smoking on duty
- Eating and drinking while on duty or in public view

- Long conversations or "gossip" with retailers, customers, or other center personnel
- Loitering around center or security office.

In addition to indicating what security officers should *not* do while on duty, you might want to include a paragraph about the type of behavior you prefer. One company includes a section saying: "Security officers and employees of the center security department while performing any security function shall be courteous and respectful in their conduct and contacts with others and shall give their name and badge number (if any) to any person who may request it."

Firearms and Other Weapons

This is an area where *it is critical to review all policies with corporate and local legal counsel and to be in full accord with your company's philosophy.* Once these requirements have been met, among the items to be considered are:

- Firearms
- Batons (straight or side-handled)
- Handcuffs
- Mace, pepper spray and other chemicals
- Knives
- Metal flashlights. (These can be used as weapons; many centers train their security people so that they will *not* use a flashlight as a weapon.)
- Stun guns. (These fire small electrodes causing an electrical shock that causes the person who has been shocked to fall to the ground.)

For each weapon:

- Who can carry it—training required, etc.
- Conditions under which it may be used
- Where it is to be stored
- How and by whom the weapon is to be maintained
- Rules for off-duty police
- Pros and cons

Equipment

Here you may want to list general guidelines for taking care of equipment. Example: Each individual is responsible for the equipment that he or she uses. This includes everything from pencil sharpeners to police vehicles and communicators. Cooperation in this respect increases our effectiveness via appearance. Both have a definite influence on us and the general public. Users of our equipment will be required to replace lost or destroyed equipment.

Or you may want to state succinctly that the security officer must check his or her personal equipment before beginning work to make sure the equipment is functional.

Some of the equipment that you might cover in this section includes:

1. Radios
2. Fire extinguishers
3. First aid kit
4. Emergency equipment
5. Keys

You may also want to consider specifying:

1. How each piece of equipment is to be used for maximum effectiveness and durability
2. Storage area and procedures for different equipment
3. Maintenance schedule and procedures for different equipment. (You may want to include or reproduce the manufacturer's suggestions here, especially if they are easy to read and understand. Otherwise you might rewrite them.)
4. What to do when equipment needs replacing.
5. Whom to report broken equipment to.

Vehicles

Vehicles are an important part of most security departments' equipment. Your security manual should indicate:

1. What types of vehicles are available, how they are marked—"Mars" lights (the flashing lights which are often mounted on a bar on the roofs of security vehicles) and/or decals—and for what purposes they should be used. The list might mention:
   a. Cars, SUVs (Sports Utility Vehicles)
   b. Jeeps
   c. Pickup trucks
   d. Scooters
   e. Golf carts
   f. Bicycles

Your security manual should indicate: What types of vehicles are available, how they are marked and for what purposes they should be used.

---

2. Rules of operation, such as:
   a. Whether the vehicle can leave the center premises for reasons other than vehicle service or maintenance
   b. How to deal with a damaged vehicle
   c. Type of fuel and where to purchase it
   d. Requirement of a driver's license, possibly in the state where the center is located
   e. The use of seat belts
   f. Treatment of all aspects of an accident
   g. Inspection of vehicle prior to use
   h. Who is allowed to ride in security vehicles
   i. A reminder to drive safely
   j. Restrictions on pursuits or chases. Example: No center vehicle is to participate in any vehicle/suspect chase that is on center property or off the center's property. If the center security vehicle participates in following a suspect, it should be under normal observing procedures, unless the vehicle is commandeered by the local law enforcement agency.

You may also consider including the use and maintenance of the following security vehicle equipment:

1. Spotlights
2. Radios
3. Fire extinguishers
4. First aid kit
5. Jump cables
6. Push bars
7. Traffic cones
8. Broom and shovel

Assisting Customers

One of the main purposes of a security department is to enhance the shopping experience of customers by helping to create a safe and comfortable shopping atmosphere. However, there may be specific times when customers ask for additional assistance, and a security manual will help security officers by spelling out the center's approved response. First you may want to indicate your philosophy. One mall manager provides that customer/tenant assistance should be managed in such a way as to achieve the following objectives:

• To ensure that all assistance is provided in a courteous, friendly, and professional manner;

- To enhance the goodwill and image of the shopping center and to maintain a pleasant shopping atmosphere;
- To conform with all local, state and federal statutes and regulations.

Some specific possibilities where customers may request assistance are dealt with by one mall manager as follows:

1. Escorts. Example: Customer escorts to and from vehicles parked outside the center should not be provided. However, the security supervisor may make exceptions to this, based on local situations.
2. Lost persons (see "Lost/Missing Persons," p. 103)
3. Lost property (see "Lost or Stolen Items," p. 109)
4. Paging. Example: Use of the center's public address system for customer assistance should be restricted to medical emergencies, lost persons or other situations as determined by the center manager.
5. Motorist assistance, including:
   a. Lockouts. Example: Security provides the service of unlocking car doors and giving jump starts at no charge. Do not accept money or other payment for this service, which is only given after the motorist has signed a Hold Harmless Agreement.
   b. Jump starts
   c. "Lost" cars
   d. Helping motorists with empty gas tanks refuel.

Assisting Tenants

As in the case of customers, a great part of a security department's routine work is done to assist retailers in the center. There are, however, special occasions when specific help is requested. One of these times might involve shoplifting, which is mentioned under both "Arrests" (p. 102) and "Theft" (p. 106) in the section on *Special Procedures*. Other occasions for helping center tenants will vary according to your corporate or local policy. Some possibilities for inclusion here are:

1. Bank escorts
2. Escorts to cars parked off center property
3. Forced entry into tenant space (which is also mentioned in the *Special Procedures* section, p. 100)

Public Release of Information

This section might be devoted to your center's broad, general policies regarding release of information to:

1. Press
2. General public

3. Agencies of city, county or state
4. Involved parties in an accident

In this section you might want to include such information as:

1. Who speaks for the center
2. Who speaks for the developer
3. Who speaks for the Merchants' Association

For example:

1. The center manager is responsible for determining which personnel at the center may release information that may affect the image and integrity of the center.
2. Requests for any information regarding center loss prevention activities are to be directed to the center's manager or to the individual designated by the manager to release information on behalf of the center.

Specific guidelines on how to release information to the public would probably be more useful if discussed in your security manual closer to the incident in question, such as the section on car accidents or the section on dealing with disasters.

Community Relations
In this section you might spell out policy, and possibly procedures too, with regard to:

1. Fire, Police and Emergency Service Departments;
2. Other municipal departments;
3. Local court.

You could address this issue in the manual by writing: The security department should establish and maintain communications and involvement with state and local community organizations and agencies to enhance the department's ability to respond to customer concerns.

Specific guidelines on how to release information to the public would probably be more useful if discussed in your security manual closer to the incident in question, such as the section on car accidents or the section on dealing with disasters.

Supporting Other Departments

The relationship between the security and maintenance departments is an important one since they interact frequently. Security also relies on the maintenance department as another set of eyes and ears.

One way to facilitate a good relationship between the departments would be to make sure that security people know the demarcations between their work and that of the maintenance department. They should also receive direction concerning how to approach the maintenance department if there is something security has noticed that requires maintenance department attention. Some possible areas are:

1. Spills
2. Litter
3. Special events
4. Roof security
5. Locks
6. Vehicle maintenance.

DAILY PROCEDURES AND POLICIES

Schedule

You may want to start this section with an overview of how the security officer's day should go, hour by hour or shift by shift. If you do, you will probably want to mention:

1. Shift change times, places and procedures
2. Shift reports and log entries
3. Patrol duties—briefly including regular activities, such as:
   a. removing parking barriers from the lot
   b. surveying parking areas for unauthorized cars
   c. supervising employee exits and store closings

Schedule: You may want to start this section with an overview of how the security officer's day should go, hour by hour or shift by shift.

---

4. Division between interior and exterior patrol time. Example: Inside patrol should encompass approximately 30% of the scheduled patrol time with the remaining 70% being outside patrol. These percentages are presented as guidelines and may vary depending on security related activity.

Patrols: General

This section may begin with some general rules that apply to both interior and exterior patrols and night and day patrols. Among the areas that might be mentioned are:

1. Reporting policy with regard to incidents or violations (such as unauthorized vehicles)
2. Whether patrol is to be individual or in pairs
3. The importance of appearance and courtesy
4. Visibility while on patrol
5. Policy with regard to establishing a patrol *routine* as opposed to a patrol that *varies* from day to day. (It should be noted that officers should not set patterns in patrol that may be detected by the criminal. Although there are certain areas that must be covered regularly, they should not be covered in the same way and at the same time on each patrol.)
6. Length of time a patrol is expected to take
7. Equipment to be carried on patrol
8. Importance of safety with regard to officer, customers and employees
9. The primary objectives of security patrols, which can be listed as:
   a. The safety and security of center patrons
   b. The observation and reportage of any dangerous or suspicious conditions
   c. Prevention of criminal acts
   d. Public relations

Patrol: Interior

You might show with a map several routes around the center interior to make clear exactly how interior and exterior patrols differ. One company discusses the following aspects of patrol and indicates center policy on each one:

1. Conditions under which security is permitted to enter retail space, e.g., shoplifting offenses, cases involving the illegal use of credit cards or checks, or other attempted larcenies
2. Lost/missing children
3. Inspection of fire extinguishers and sprinkler system
4. Trash and spills

> *Your security manual might show a map with several routes around the center interior to make clear exactly how interior and exterior patrols differ.*

5. Blocked service corridors
6. Periodic check of rest rooms
7. Loitering groups or individuals
8. Roof leaks and other building damage to which the maintenance department should be alerted
9. Bus stops
10. Truck tunnels and stairwells
11. Prevention of loud noise (which might be handled this way: "Prohibit anyone carrying a portable radio or recorder from playing it on center property. Usually a polite request is sufficient; however, if the request is not obeyed, the individual shall be escorted from center property. If a loud noise emanates from a store [stereos, televisions, radios, electronic games, etc.], the condition should be immediately reported to management.")

Patrol: Exterior
Under this heading you might repeat some of the center's policies with regard to vehicle use and care.

In this section you may indicate *where* the patrol should cover, including possibly:

- Inner roads
- Outer roads
- Docking areas
- Loading zones
- Outer perimeter of parking lot
- Fire lanes
- Doors to center (when it is closed)
- Outside lighting

Then indicate *what* the patrolling officer is to be looking for, including such things as:

- Anything "abnormal"
- Abandoned vehicles
- Illegally parked cars and trucks
- Tow trucks
- Persons attempting to enter a vehicle
- Persons stripping vehicles
- Purse snatchers
- Muggers
- Hazards and other unsafe conditions

- Fire and maintenance problems
- Burned-out lights (at night)
- Locked corridors and dock doors, when appropriate
- Employees walking to and from cars.

Then you might tell *how* to respond, i.e., what procedures should be used when any of the conditions listed above are found. This could include:

- Getting help
- Calling the supervisor
- Use of the radio
- When to call the police
- Restriction on use of vehicles for chase
- Issuing of "courtesy" or warning parking tickets.

During the daily patrol, the security officer may hear complaints from tenants. You might want to indicate here how these complaints are to be handled.

Night Patrol/Security

This section might indicate how the center is to be secured at night, including procedures and personnel involved.

If the center has a night patrol, this section should indicate:

1. Number and routes of tours to be made
2. Reporting procedures for normal and abnormal occurrences
3. Training for alarm systems
4. What to look for, including, possibly:
   a. Fires
   b. Trespassers
   c. Unsafe conditions
   d. Power failures caused by weather and other conditions
   e. Door security of stores
   f. Strange noises
   g. Cars left in parking lot overnight
   h. Condition of lighting
   j. Who to call if help is needed.

Night Patrol: *This section of the manual might include the number and routes of tours to be made and the reporting procedures for normal and abnormal occurrences.*

Center Retailer Openings and Closings
Among the items in this section you might include:

1. Procedures for opening and closing the center
2. Who is responsible for each aspect of opening and closing the center
3. Any log notations or reports that must be filed

Since security may be involved with this aspect of center operation, or may become involved if there is a problem, you should indicate here policies and procedures with regard to opening and closing the center and the shops of its tenant retailers.

Door Security and Lighting
A retailer's door open after hours can be a sign of trouble. Here you might want to indicate what to do when that occurs, including:

1. Who to call:
   a. Police
   b. Retailer emergency contact
   c. Center management
2. How to close the door
3. Policy on entering the store, if that is necessary

   Your policy discussion on lighting might include:

1. Lights for which security patrol is reponsible:
   a. Exterior
   b. Interior
2. How often lights should be checked
3. To whom reports of nonfunctioning lights should be made

EMPLOYEE PARKING

Most shopping centers have designated certain areas for employee parking. These areas are usually less convenient than spaces reserved for customers because convenient parking is a strong drawing factor for a center. Security departments are usually involved in enforcing the rules with regard to employee parking. Part of the policy may be to make sure that all center employees abide by employee parking rules. Another part may be that consistent violators be noted and their actions discussed with their employer(s). There may also be a towing policy and a notification procedure before that policy is put into effect.

Check with your legal counsel for the difference between designating areas for employees to park and designating areas where employees are not allowed to park. Tenant leases should also be consulted for employee parking provisions.

SPECIAL PROCEDURES

REPORTS

Most special procedures, such as those discussed below, require that reports be filed indicating what happened and what action was taken. While noting the need for reports here, you might also at the same time *give the reason* for the paperwork. It is also a good idea to mention the reporting procedure each time the specific type of incident is discussed in the manual and then to summarize all uses of a particular report at the place in the manual where all the possible reports and their uses are described.

Among the reports most commonly used by shopping centers are the following:

1. Incident report and supplemental report
2. Personal injury report (may be done on the incident report)
3. Officer's activity log (outlines the time, location and activity of each officer during his/her shift)
4. Liability release (for medical aid, jump starts or unlocking vehicles)
5. Shift or summary report (used to record incidents for review by management and/or other officers)
6. Training log (showing the time, date and type of training received)
7. Tenant information list (emergency phone numbers of tenants)

There are many other possible reports designed for specific tasks. Based on the needs of your center, you may want to include some of the following:

1. Monthly incident summary report (compilation of all activity by catergory and number)
2. Bomb threat (telephone log of the threat)
3. Terrorist threat precautionary procedures (based on U.S. Department of Homeland Security alert level advisories)
4. Fire report (actual fire; may be done on the incident report)
5. Access log (for access to restricted areas)
6. Center event notice (from marketing or center management)
7. Property receipt (for lost or found)
8. Uniform/equipment (inventory or checkout)
9. Lockers (condition of, etc.)
10. Coin collection (fountain)

11. Fire extinguisher log
12. Vehicle impound (towing)
13. Tenant fire/safety inspection
14. Tenant lease violation
15. Late opening/early closing
16. Lost and found donation
17. Employment background check release
18. Center parking ticket
19. Auto accident
20. Witness statement
21. Vehicle use
22. Dispatch log
23. Emergency telephone list
24. Subjects arrested or banned list
25. Factory Mutual Sprinkler Control (forms)
26. Riser room condition (sprinkler)
27. Roof access log
28. Refusal of medical assistance
29. Key control log
30. Release of information
31. Report retention
32. Distribution and flow

Personal Accidents/First Aid

If someone has an accident in the center, members of the security department may become involved in providing help. Among the items that can guide their actions are discussions of:

1. Appropriate training required before first aid or cardiopulmonary resuscitation (CPR) may be administered
2. Legal aspects of giving first aid
3. Location of first aid kits
4. Procedures to be followed when first aid is needed (e.g., when a person is to be moved, how reassurance that help is on the way is to be given, how to communicate with emergency personnel)
5. Enlistment of help from outside sources (e.g., police or fire or emergency medical services)
6. Required reports

A detailed definition of first aid should also be included. Such a definition might be:

1. Immediate temporary care
2. Given by a trained person
3. In case of sudden illness or accident
4. Before medical assistance is available
5. To prevent death or further injury and to relieve pain or counteract shock

You may wish to provide a special reminder to security officers, such as this: "Remember to be prompt in communicating, clear when requesting assistance, exact when giving location, and calm and reassuring."

Vehicle Accidents

Many of the same procedures apply when dealing with a vehicle accident as with a personal accident. In addition, you might ask the parties if they wish the police to investigate.

Arrests

Developers, managers, and local political entities should have definite policies with regard to arrests on center or private property, and this section should be written with the advice of your company's legal and policy-setting departments, and then reviewed by local counsel.

You might begin this section by defining arrest, as written in the local statutes, such as: "An arrest is made by an actual restraint of the person to be arrested, or by his submission to the custody of the person making the arrest." Your local statutes will differ in wording, although the basic idea will probably be the same.

> *Developers, managers, and local political entities should have definite policies with regard to arrests on center or private property, and it is crucial that this section be written with the advice of your company's legal and policy-setting departments, and then reviewed by local counsel.*

Then you might spell out clearly your center's or ownership's policy. For example, whether there are incidents and/or times arrests will be made or whether to hold or detain someone on the word of someone else.

In some centers, for employees to effect an arrest, the incident must have happened to an employee and/or involving center property. Some employee must have witnessed the incident. In those states that allow you to arrest for probable cause, you should be extremely careful, and arrests should only be made in clear cases.

Anytime an arrest or a detention pursuant to an arrest is effected, call the police. Whenever possible, turn everything over to the police and let them take over and make the actual arrest. One can serve as a witness and/or sign the complaint when necessary.

This section might include:

1. Legal aspects (as discussed above)
2. When an arrest can be made by security personnel, if at all
3. Procedure for making an arrest or a citizen's arrest
4. Involvement with and/or cooperation with the police
5. Role of security in cases of shoplifting. Example: As a general rule, any report of shoplifting in a retail establishment should be handled carefully. A security officer not witnessing the theft is not allowed to arrest a reported shoplifter. The person who observed the theft must make the arrest.
6. Rearrest in case of escape
7. Notification of judicial authority
8. Notification of people within your corporation and/or center hierarchy
9. Policy with regard to use of force

Lost/Missing Persons

Missing persons usually involve children. You can state your policy succinctly. Example: "All lost persons are to be reported to the center office. All possible assistance is to be provided in locating lost persons."

You may, however, take a different approach and talk specifically about lost children, indicating that they:

1. Should not be walked through the center looking for their parents
2. Should instead be taken immediately to the center office
3. The center office should call the police and inform them of the details

When children are reported as missing, your policy might be to:

1. Ascertain the facts as to place and time last seen, plus physical description of the missing child
2. Dispatch all information to center personnel
3. Assign specific areas to look (e.g., stairwells, restrooms, service corridors, vacant tenant spaces, storage areas, etc.)
4. Use security vehicles to look in perimeter areas and shrubs and bushes
5. Notify police

Further advisement might read: Remember! *If there is an abduction, the first few minutes are crucial to recovery.* All employees must be made aware of the sensitivity and importance of the situation and must be directed to refer all inquiries to the person designated for that purpose.

Alarms

It is likely that there are both *center* and *retailer* alarms for both fire and intrusion, and that the procedures for dealing with each type when they sound may vary. Indicate—among other things—for each alarm, where appropriate:

1. Alarm location
2. Setting and resetting procedure
3. Who to contact when it sounds, i.e., center policy with regard to tenant alarms
4. What to do if store personnel are unavailable
5. Involvement with local law enforcement or fire agency
6. Dealing with false alarms

Dealing with Center Personnel

Most security departments have a communications system whereby officers can communicate with each other and with other people in center management. The section discussing this system might include:

List of equipment available, and for each type of equipment:

a. Who is authorized to use it
b. When it should be used
c. Where equipment is stored
d. Maintenance required for equipment
e. What to do in case of breakage or other damage
f. Operating instructions for equipment (perhaps from manufacturer if clear and easy to understand)
g. How the equipment should be used. (For example, your security manual may say, "Radios are to be used only when it is necessary to communicate with another unit or the base station. At all times the officer's radio should be turned on, with the volume at a reasonable level so transmissions can be heard by the officer but not by the general public.")
h. The use and meaning of any letter or number codes in use at the center
j. Paging (when it can be done to assist a customer and when it can be done to locate a center or retail employee)

Crimes Against Persons

If your shopping center has special policies dealing with crimes against persons, they should be stated here. Otherwise you might just note that crimes against persons do occasionally occur in centers and that the arrest procedures previously described apply when they do.

Vandalism

When center or retail property has been damaged, there are several possible courses of action open to a security department. Some issues that might be raised in this section include:

1. Use of photographs
2. Differentiation between damage done to center property and damage done to a retailer's property
3. When and how to involve the police department
4. Correcting the problem (probably involving the maintenance department)
5. Required reports
6. Reference to the manual's section on arrests

Parking Lot Assistance

Most shopping centers have policies regarding helping motorists with:

- Locked vehicles
- "Lost" vehicles
- Jump starts
- Calling emergency services for towing, etc.

These policies, which should be stated here, may include having the motorist sign a Release of Liability, which can be defined in the manual as a written waiver of liability releasing any and all claims for negligence and damage to the security officer, his/her employer and the owner and operator of the center for the assistance rendered.

Policy may also require the motorist to give evidence of ownership before assistance is given. Further, a report, which may include the signed waiver or Release of Liability, may be required each time a motorist is helped.

Part of the policy may also reflect the center's attitude toward tips. For instance, you might instruct security officers not to accept money or other payment for unlocking doors and giving jump starts, which are often provided at no charge to center customers.

Towing Vehicles

Among the items to be covered in this section are:

1. Circumstances under which vehicle will be towed
2. Attempted notification of vehicle owner

3. Conformity with state and local statutes (including proper signage)
4. Cooperation with law enforcement agencies
5. Responsibility for payment of towing charges
6. Any required reports

Theft

Since protection of property is one of the missions of the security department, its members are involved with cases involving theft. These may be divided into two groups:

1. Theft of center property, e.g., vehicles or maintenance equipment.
2. Shoplifting from the shopping center's retailers.

The policies for dealing with each kind of theft may differ.
    Some of the relevant concerns are:

1. Legal, i.e., power of arrest (see "Arrests," p. 102)
2. Center policy on detention, especially with regard to a crime the security officer may not have witnessed firsthand
3. How security may cooperate with merchants when retail theft occurs
4. Required reports
5. Differentiation of shoplifting from creating a public disturbance in the center
6. Involvement of police
7. General policy can state: "We do not make arrests of shoplifters or people causing a verbal disturbance for tenants. This includes any type of detention, handcuffing, transporting, interviewing, questioning or searches of shoplifters. Only the tenant can do this. If a disturbance is caused by a shoplifter in the common area of the center, we can take action; but only because of the disturbance, *not* the shoplifting act."

Trespassing Violations

Trespassing may be divided into two different types:

1. Being in certain "off-limits" places—meter rooms, maintenance rooms, etc.—at any time
2. Being in other places, such as the center interior, at certain inappropriate times, such as after mall hours

An example of trespassing policy used by one center consists of the following: If the person has violated a center rule or law of the city or state, that person should be removed. If there has been a violation, do the following:

1. Stop the individual and identify yourself as center security.
2. Advise the person of his violation and ask him to leave.
3. If the person refuses, advise him that you will notify the police to have them assist.
4. If the person still refuses, leave the immediate area and wait a few minutes (often the person will leave).
5. If the person still remains, stand by him as though you are waiting for the police (again, often the person will leave).
6. If the person still refuses to leave, contact the police.
7. Upon arrival of the police, inform them of the violation(s) and allow them to do their function.
8. The time and date of the notification of trespassing must be documented.

The manual can continue: If the individual does not violate a center rule, observe his actions and be visible to him. This will usually be sufficient for attaining his departure off center property. Do not, however, give him any cause for undesirable reactions as he and you are in the public eye. Use common sense.

Demonstrations/Labor Disputes
Local counsel must determine the state law on public demonstrations in shopping centers. A few states require large malls to allow this activity under reasonable regulations of time, place, and manner. Most states permit the center to adopt the policy its management determines is best. One way to word a general policy statement with regard to public demonstrations may be: "The question of deciding whether a strike, public demonstration, handbilling or solicitation is permitted in a center or in the parking lot, and, if so, the reasonable time, place and manner restrictions must be made by the center manager; it should not be decided by security. Security's role is to see that participants do not interfere with persons entering or leaving the center, comply with the restrictions imposed on their access, and otherwise act in an orderly fashion, in keeping with the center's rules."
In addition to general policy, some specific areas to be covered might include:

1. Notification of developer/manager headquarters if strike is pending
2. Notification and updating of headquarters and regional offices
3. Insistence on center management's obligation and responsibility to make certain that this labor matter does not disrupt the orderly operation of the center

Unsecured Doors
Most centers have a policy of requesting that retailers notify center management when someone has been authorized by the tenant to be in their space after the center has closed. The names of the authorized people are kept on a list in the

center office. Security should be made aware of this list, and night patrols should check it before beginning their rounds.

When a night patrol finds a retailer's door that is open, the patrol must consider several things:

1. Notification of responsible retailer personnel by using emergency list in center office.
2. The possibility that there is a theft taking place
3. Involvement of the police
4. Locking the door, including:
   a. Taping the door to alert patrol to further entries or exits of the premises
   b. Later notifying the tenant—assumed to be unreachable when unsecured door was discovered—as to what was done

Forced Entry

In this section, you might address:

1. Situations in which security might need to gain forced entry to a locked tenant space
2. Qualifications needed to make forced entry so as to deal with an emergency situation
3. What to do in case of fire

Roof Access

Because many centers have had problems with unauthorized people gaining access to the roof, they have developed policies to deal with roof access. In a manual, some items to be covered might include:

1. Reasons for limiting roof access
2. Keys required to reach roof
3. Reports required to gain access to the roof
4. Check-in and check-out procedures for roof workers
5. Rules for using the roof (e.g., all work must be cleaned up or person will be denied access in the future)

Contractors' Common Area Access

Occasionally, work in tenant space will require a contractor to utilize common area space while the work is being done. This might be regulated by rules covering the following areas:

1. Listing of prohibited and permitted work
2. Specifications for making sure that tenant work does not make an unsightly area in the center (barricades, etc.)

3. Protection and restoration of all center property, especially neutral piers and soffits
4. Trash handling
5. Behavior of workers (loud music, attire, etc.)
6. Use by workers of public restrooms.

Lost or Stolen Items

Security will get involved when customers report items lost or stolen. Procedures will usually involve:

1. A report including basic information on the complainant and the missing item
2. Communicating the information to appropriate center personnel
3. Center policy with regard to helping persons locate items can state: "Assistance will be provided in searching for lost property, except for property reported lost in tenant spaces."

Found Items

Items found by center personnel or customers or tenants will also need special procedures, possibly including, among others:

1. Inventory, tagging, and identification of found object
2. Notification of owner, if possible
3. Storage
4. Disposal of unclaimed items

Fire Inspections

Although the local fire department will probably be involved in fire inspections, if your center expects security personnel to help with the job by performing their own inspections, this subject should be in your manual, including:

1. How often inspections are to be made
2. What inspection should involve
3. What forms are to be filled out and filed

Checks/Credit Cards

Center policies differ as to whether security guards become involved in cases of bad checks or forged credit cards which have been used for purchases from retailers. Your policy should be spelled out, either here, in a separate section, or in the section on theft (see "Theft," p. 106).

Special Events

If your shopping center may be the site of special, community-wide events, you might want to include in the manual:

1. Description of possible events
2. Expected behavior of participants—mentioning controlled substances, attire, etc.
3. Procedures to help prepare for and clean up from the event
4. Chain of command during the event
5. Any required reports.

EMERGENCY/DISASTER/TERRORIST THREAT PROCEDURES

Centers consider procedures for all or some of the following:

- Earthquakes
- Fires
- Floods
- Power failures
- Hurricanes
- Tornadoes
- Inclement weather
- Bomb threats, terrorist threats
- Shootings and any other acts of violence
- Acts of terrorism

The security department will have an important role to play when and if any of these events occur. Each individual manual should detail who is in charge during a disaster or an emergency and exactly what role security will play in each situation, whether it is cleaning up from a storm or evacuating the public from a bomb threat situation.

What follows in this *Guide to Writing a Shopping Center Security Manual* is a general listing of many of the topics that should be covered when instructing security personnel on how the center should deal with both natural and man-made emer-

> *Each individual manual should detail who is in charge during a disaster and exactly what role security will play in each situation.*

gencies and disasters. In your own manual you may be more specific. You may also find it more useful *to detail the procedures for each possibility separately*. Although this will involve a lot of repetition since many of the procedures will be the same, it may make the manual more useful. If you do it this way, anyone consulting the manual in an emergency will be reading a step-by-step outline in which everything that is written pertains to their immediate situation, and they will not be required—under time pressure—to sift out the steps that do not apply to their particular situation or turn back and forth to different sections.

This section—or sections—dealing with emergencies and disasters should receive particular attention from both *local and home office counsel,* as well as from *top officers of the company,* to make sure it is in compliance with all laws, ordinances and corporate policies.

Local fire, police and other municipal departments should also get involved in formulating the procedures for this section. Procedures at the center must not only conform to local laws, they must also take into account what the local authorities will and will not do to help out in an emergency. You must know, for instance, in the case of a bomb threat, whether the police department will send equipment and/or officers to the scene so that you know what the center's responsibilities will be.

In modern society, perils can take many forms and come from many sources. September 11th has taught all free societies to be on guard. Centers in the United States may want to be mindful of the national threat level alert status issued by the U.S. Department of Homeland Security to guard against terrorist attacks. Centers in other countries may monitor their own official sources as well. The center itself has to determine what measures are appropriate, depending on the center's location and special circumstances, as it relates to the announced threat level, which can be included as part of the center's security manual.

Since security and other personnel will be reading this section under pressure, as well as at a calmer time when it has been used as a training tool, it is absolutely essential that it be written in a *clear and easy-to-understand manner,* perhaps stressing lists and phrases over paragraphs and sentences.

The pages in the security manual devoted to Emergency and Disaster Procedures will probably differ from other sections of the manual in this way: Other sections dealt exclusively with the responsibilities of the security department; this section will probably deal with the activities of everyone in center management, and possibly even with what tenants, government agencies and home office personnel will be required to do. *Instead of stressing security's unique responsibilities, it will probably indicate where security fits into a total picture of center activity to deal with the emergency, always indicating who is giving the directions in any situation.*

Another possibility is to have two emergency plans—one as part of the security manual detailing all of security's duties and actions, and a second one which outlines the entire emergency plan with each department's activities in a separate section. In fact, the security section of this "Emergency Manual" could also go into the security manual.

At some point, either before or after you have listed the detailed emergency procedures, you may want to make a list of "Do's and Don't's for Disaster Recovery." One center manager's list includes:

Do . . .
- *Keep employees informed of conditions and extent of recovery. Tell them when you expect to call them back and on what basis.*
- *Try to return to normal operations as soon as possible to minimize the extraordinary responsibilities on personnel.*
- *Encourage imagination. Only real ingenuity will solve many of the problems. Show appreciation for effort.*

Don't . . .
- *Jump to conclusions based on hearsay. If time doesn't permit thorough checking, at least get some facts before making important decisions.*
- *Be over-critical of people and work. All of you will be anxious, tired and tense.*
- *Lift emergency precautions too soon. Recovery to 100% safe conditions takes longer than you might think.*

Policy

This section might begin with a statement of policy, such as: "To establish a formal plan of action to minimize the danger to life, health and property from emergencies or disasters, and to take necessary and prudent steps to assure continuity of operations and restoration of normal business activities."

Your policy statement might be written this way: The center manager's main concerns in any emergency situation shall be:

1. The safety of center patrons, employees and the center
2. The protection of property
3. The security and preservation of company documents
4. An accurate reporting of the details pertaining to the emergency

Deployment of Personnel

In an emergency people must know:

1. Location and telephone number of command center
2. Chain of command, including authority of:
    a. Center personnel
    b. Home office departments and their telephone numbers
    c. Police and fire departments and their telephone numbers. (It can be helpful to print this information on a wallet-sized card and distribute it to all center personnel.)

3. Location of shelter areas, emergency generators, etc. (You may wish to provide several maps in this section of the manual.)
4. Specific responsibilities of different departments, perhaps indicated on a chart
5. As part of this section:
    a. Who makes the decision about clearing the center
    b. Who makes the decision to reopen the center
    c. Who makes the decision to evacuate

Evacuation

In an emergency situation, clearly indicate:

1. Who decides if the center is to be evacuated
2. Steps to take in an evacuation
3. Identification and access of personnel allowed into the center after it has been evacuated
4. Announcements over the public address system may state: "Attention please. In cooperation with police and fire departments, we are conducting an evacuation of the center. All persons are asked to leave the building immediately via the nearest exit. Center personnel will help direct you to the exit doors. Thank you."
5. Searching for people unable to leave on their own—handicapped or injured
6. Map of evacuation routes.

Documentation of Events

For insurance and other purposes, as soon as the immediate danger is past, you will probably want a record of what has happened. This may be done via:

1. Reports
2. Photographs, including aerial photographs
3. Ledgers of expenses during the emergency

Center Communication

You might consider addressing the following items in this section:

1. How to communicate if a power failure makes the public address system inoperable
2. Cooperation with center anchor stores
3. What will be required of all tenants in an emergency
4. Notifying the home office about the emergency—when and whom to notify
5. Getting in touch with insurance companies
6. The possibility of installing extra phone lines dedicated to coping with the emergency

7. Points center personnel and tenants should know, such as:
   a. Condition, cause, and time frame of emergency, if possible
   b. Who is in charge and the entire chain of command
   c. Location of shelter areas
   d. Evacuation procedures
   e. Who will conduct searches for missing persons

Working with Local Officials

In this section you might consider indicating who will communicate with each different segment of the community, guidelines for what will be said, and methods of reaching them in an emergency, which should include the telephone numbers of:

1. Police Department
2. Fire Department
3. Power Company
4. Water Company
5. Emergency medical services
6. Red Cross
7. Media. (You might want to lay down some general guidelines. Examples: Refrain from commenting on the extent of damage, injuries, dollar amounts, etc., until a complete assessment can be made. Be sensitive to the center's image and the local community concerns. Volunteer documented facts to the media to help dispel rumors and misstatements.)

Protecting Property

Once the security personnel are certain they have done everything possible to assure the safety and/or comfort of center employees and customers, they can take action to ensure that center property is protected from vandals. This is the section where you might outline what mechanical and human steps you will take to make sure that property damage is as slight as possible.

Power Failures

In this discussion you might consider listing the following items:

1. Sources and activation of auxiliary power
2. Restoring power
3. Substitutions for power (e.g., how to notify the public if the public address system does not work)

Training for Emergencies

In order to make sure that emergencies and disasters are handled well, the center should probably run regular drills. Security could be important in implementing this policy, and its role should be spelled out in the manual. At the time of the drills, all lists of phone numbers, personnel, and maps might be updated.

After the Danger Is Past
Among the items you might deal with here are:

1. Assessing the damage
2. Maintaining a photo record of the situation
3. How to enlist tenant cooperation in repairs
4. Cleaning up
5. Priorities for restoration
6. Sources—local tradespeople and suppliers, etc.—for repair of center property
7. Whether there will be temporary changes in center policy so tenant and center reconstruction can proceed most efficiently. (This may include changes in opening and closing hours; security's role in carrying out the changes must be listed clearly here.)

12 | The Reality of Potential Terrorism at Shopping Centers

The increasing number of domestic and international terrorist attacks continually reported by the media throughout the late 1980s and 1990s even until today has heightened the public's awareness of our vulnerability to future attacks almost anywhere. The 1993 World Trade Center bombing, the bombing of the Alfred P. Murrah Federal Building in Oklahoma City in April 1995, the July 1996 Centennial Olympic Park bombing, the Pan American Flight 103 tragedy over Lockerbie, Scotland, and the September 11, 2001 World Trade Center attack are just of few of the many and varied terrorist actions that have instilled fear in people around the world. Terrorists have demonstrated that they will attack in many ways and will direct their horror against a broad range of targets. Terrorists have no regard for human life or property; in fact, we often see them take their own lives to accomplish their mission of fear and terror.

The government defines terrorism as the "unlawful use of force or violence, committed by a group(s) or two or more individuals, against persons or property to intimidate or coerce a government, the civilian population, or any segment thereof, in furtherance of political or social objectives." In short, terrorists want to disrupt our way of life by instilling fear, eliminating or drastically affecting our freedom, creating a lack of confidence in our government, and negatively affecting our economy. Terror attacks on many different types of public access targets can successfully accomplish the terrorist's objectives. Because the shopping center and/or retail environment maintains a high profile in the community, is normally heavily populated with civilians (shoppers), is a vital part of our economy, and symbolizes the freedom we enjoy in our everyday life in America, it becomes a potential target for terrorist attack.

In considering terrorist actions at shopping centers along with the resulting security responses, we can look to the country of Israel, where terrorists consistently attack, or attempt to attack, shopping centers with suicide bombers wounding and killing numbers of innocent citizens.

In a presentation to the International Council of Shopping Centers—Security Conference in Chicago (2002) Arik Arad, former Israeli intelligence officer and head of shopping center security for that country, explained that Israeli shopping centers are protected by exterior vehicle and customer searches and paramilitary security officers patrolling the interior and exterior of malls with long-barreled weapons. Dogs trained to detect the presence of explosives have also been deployed at the exterior of centers in Israel. In his position as chief of security for all shopping centers in Israel, Mr. Arad was consistently privy to sensitive military intelligence regarding known or suspected bombers as they moved about in the country. Centers were often forewarned regarding terrorists intending to come onto shopping center property. So good was the Israeli intelligence along with the unconventional security measures that during a ten (10)-year period only four (4) of one hundred (100) suicide bombers even made it beyond the entry of a mall to detonate their bombing devices. This saved many lives.

Mr. Arad suggested that management, tenants and customers initially resisted these unconventional security measures and controls but grew to accept them after terror attacks that resulted in the loss of many lives at shopping centers within Israel. Had the suicide bomber(s) made it into the common area of the mall, many more lives would have been claimed. In the face of these drastic security measures, Israeli malls continue to be targets of terrorist attacks. Upon examining the actions and responses that occurred in Israel, it becomes apparent that it is virtually impossible to prevent all acts of terrorism in open accessible environments.

Despite the fear and anxiety that linger in the hearts and minds of the American people following the terrorist attack on the World Trade Center in September 2001, our culture is not prepared to accept the extreme security measures used at shopping centers in Israel. Understanding that shopping centers are only one of the many kinds of public-access properties that terrorists may target to accomplish their goals, and remaining sensitive to the reluctance of the typical U.S. retail patron, shopping center management has been challenged to develop a less radical safety and security response for their property.

The creation of a four (4)-part Crisis Readiness Plan that responds to various threat levels published by the Department of Homeland Security and enhances security controls and measures proportionate to the alert status through the use of a predetermined continuum may be helpful in addressing potential terrorist action while, at the same time, establishing reasonable emergency responses.

A suggested four (4)-part Crisis Readiness Plan may include:

1. Threat Verification Process
2. Threat-Level-Based Incident Response Continuum

3. Emergency Management Program
4. Business Resumption Plan

1. THREAT VERIFICATION PROCESS

This aspect of the Crisis Readiness Plan provides a listing of actions that may be taken to insure that management is continually aware of the most current intelligence regarding the level of readiness that may be instituted at the property. A sample listing of some suggested steps follows:

- Daily review of Department of Homeland Security internet site noting threat level color code and/or additional information
- Verify threat information or intelligence with state and local agencies
- Network with other industry contacts (other community retail centers)
- Contact other private security sources such as ASIS, ICSC, Truth or Fiction.com, etc.
- Meet with property management to discuss threat level assessment decisions
- Communicate with corporate level management and/or retained security consultant

Decisions regarding security responses to a published elevated threat level should consider the nature and detail of intelligence that accompanies the elevated level. It is possible that the intelligence that caused the elevated threat level may be industry- or area (geographic)-specific, which may affect decisions associated with your response.

2. THREAT-LEVEL-BASED INCIDENT RESPONSE CONTINUUM

A threat-level-based response continuum consists of a predetermined menu of potential actions that may be taken by management based upon the published threat level and local intelligence. Management may elect to institute all or any number of the pre-listed procedures or measures based upon the detail of the intelligence data. This advanced listing is meant to assist in making emergency management decisions that may have to be made under stressful conditions.

Threat Level—Green
Normal operating procedures, no actual or perceived threats or events. Management, Operations, Security, Maintenance, Housekeeping, Customer Service, tenants and parking operations will operate under normal conditions with no specific measures or controls.

Threat Level—Blue

A heightened security awareness should exist within all operations based on any nonspecific or general threat received from law enforcement or an intelligence agency. Specific operational and security measures will be established while operating at this threat level. Examples of operational adjustments may include enhanced regulation of the loading dock areas, closer supervision of contractors entering and working at the property, and strict control of rooftop access.

Threat Level—Yellow

This is a higher alert level based on specific intelligence regarding threats to public-access facilities wherein shopping centers or large retail environments are included as potential targets. This elevated alert status may be instituted if the intelligence includes details regarding methods and/or types of actions and the focus of the intelligence and threat specifies your geographic region of the country. Responses taken may include all or some of the following:

- Meet with all department heads to discuss plans and measures
- Meet with representatives of local utilities, systems contractors
- Meet with lead security personnel — discuss additional staffing and deployment adjustments
- Contact local police, fire and emergency services
- Limit access to loading docks. Prohibit nonessential contractors from working on property.
- Detailed searches of all delivery vehicles entering the property
- Establish search stations at all entrances to the mall. Search bags, packages, backpacks, etc.
- Insure all roof accesses are locked. Limit number of persons authorized to open rooftop access doors.
- Escort all essential contractors to electrical rooms, pump stations, mechanical rooms, etc.
- Establish stationary posts at key areas of the property (HVAC, electrical, gas, water)
- Limit parking areas—insure a safe zone immediately adjacent to the perimeter of the building
- Contact public transportation department if evacuation may become necessary

Threat Level—Orange

This is an elevated threat level based on specific verified intelligence information indicating a possible terrorist action directed at shopping centers or large retail environments. This elevated alert status may be instituted if the intelligence includes details regarding methods and/or types of actions and the focus of the intelligence and threat specifies your geographic region of the country. Responses taken may include all or some of the following. Responses may include all or a portion of the planned responses taken from blue, yellow or red levels:

- Contact predetermined law enforcement sources to verify the exact nature and level of the threat.
- Increase physical security levels throughout the property [interior and exterior].
- Ensure mechanical rooms are locked down.
- Move unattended vehicles away from the building perimeter.
- Establish fixed security posts at loading docks.
- Prohibit patrons from carrying backpacks onto the property.
- Deploy stricter property sinage.
- Meet with department heads and direct tenant representatives to effect higher security practices.

Threat Level—Red

This is the highest level of threat. If declared it would result in a business and building shutdown. In order for a Red Threat Level to be declared, intelligence concerning a possible terrorist action would be site-specific, including time and method of attack. Red level could be declared if a neighboring property were named as a target.

Examples of actions that may be taken in the event of a red threat level may include:

- Coordinate efforts with all local public safety officials.
- Initiate evacuation procedures as required (refer to evacuation plan within Emergency and Disaster Planning Management).
- Complete lockdown of the entire property, including each tenant space.
- Utilize locks and chains on doors as required and available.
- Blockade all parking area entrances with jersey barriers or similar barricade.
- Restrict all access to essential personnel and public safety officials. Require ID.
- Coordinate efforts with all utilities.
- Activate an off-site command post. Follow Emergency and Disaster Planning and Management.

To be sure, the previously suggested actions may not be all-inclusive or appropriate for each and every property. As has been emphasized throughout this text, security and emergency management controls and measures may vary considerably based on the many factors defined in the "Step One" process.

3. EMERGENCY MANAGEMENT PROGRAM

In the event your center is victimized by a terrorist action, it is suggested that you follow appropriate action steps for the type of attack outlined in the Emergency and Disaster Planning and Management.

4. BUSINESS RESUMPTION PLAN

The business resumption plan lists a series of steps property owners/managers may want to consider taking as they begin recovering from a terrorist action:

➤ Conduct follow-up intelligence from recognized sources to determine viability of resuming business.
➤ Examine the effected area for structural integrity.
➤ Coordinate with building inspectors, engineers, and contractors for appropriate maintenance and repair.
➤ Examine and repair all mechanicals, utilities and safety systems.
➤ Insure compliance with city and state inspection requirements.
➤ Create safe, unobstructed ingress and egress for tenants, vendors, customers and vehicles.
➤ Develop and display proper informational and directional signage appropriate for reopening.
➤ Determine the published threat level and verify.
➤ Insure the safety of tenants, employees, vendors, and customers.

ADDITIONAL OPERATIONAL AND PROCEDURAL CONSIDERATIONS

The following is a laundry list of additional considerations that may be discussed and considered in compiling a more comprehensive listing of potential proactive and responsive measures to be included in your incident response continuum. These considerations are listed by category or department and may not be all-inclusive or appropriate for your property:

Mall Management
Inform and involve all mall staff members
Training and planning for potential disasters or emergencies
Conduct live emergency drills
Conduct table-top drills and review emergency procedures

Public Relations Issues

Assist mall management with release of plans and information to tenants

Assist with media issues

Discuss press releases regarding threat responses

Issues associated with business resumption after critical incident

Leasing and Specialty Leasing Personnel

Consider background checks regarding potential tenants

Remain alert to unusual tenant activity

Establish heightened awareness for intelligence information associated with particular merchandise lines

Operations and Maintenance

Structural and mechanical hardening

Protection of critical mechanical and utility functions (HVAC, electric, gas, water)

Restrict access to identified areas

Review emergency procedures and plans

Establish communication with public utility agencies

Security Operations

Emergency training and planning

Staffing and deployment (contingency)

Access control(s)

Search of persons and packages

Reporting and follow-up regarding suspicious persons and incidents

Photographing and filming restrictions and procedures

Disseminating critical information to tenants, employees, and customers

Loading dock operations (access controls, ID of vendor)

Review and train emergency procedures and plans

Conduct live and/or table-top drills

Housekeeping Operations

Awareness of abandoned or unattended packages

Reporting procedures regarding suspicious activity or incidents

Review of emergency procedures

Parking Operations

Identification and reporting abandoned or unknown vehicles

Reporting suspicious activity or incidents

Access control and/or closing parking sectors or entire lot/deck
Review emergency procedures associated with vehicles

Communications
Review communications procedures established in Emergency and Disaster Planning and Management
Designate command post and alternate off-site command post

Liaison Functions
Local and/or combined police task force
Police, fire and emergency services
U.S Attorney's Office (Counter Terrorism Representative)
F.B.I. and other Federal Agencies
Public Transportation Dept.

Tenant Relations & Communications
Identify and relay threat level changes to tenants
Use and testing of center's telephone system
Distribution of informational and instructional material
Education and training regarding evacuation

TRAINING AND ADVANCED PREPARATION CONSIDERATIONS

Training
First aid and disaster management for security and staff
First responder, officer survival and defense for security officers
Deployment exercises (live)
Evacuation drills involving staff and tenants (nonbusiness hours)
Live disaster drills with staff and public safety agencies

Advanced Preparation Considerations
Insure complete inventory of first aid kits
Develop and purchase signage for identified security checkpoints/control areas
Develop and purchase signage for parking lot controls
Assemble supply locker for off-site emergency management location

Consider including:
    Emergency management plans with contact numbers
    Property and building plans

Area maps
Telephone book(s)
Pens, paper, clipboards
Binoculars, flashlights, bottled water
Spare handheld radio(s) with batteries
Cell phone—spare batteries and/or charger
AM/FM radio
First aid kit
Protective clothing [safety glasses, helmet(s), gloves, etc.]
Portable generator with fuel

A Crisis Readiness Plan should be created with the understanding that if terrorists target your property for an attack, the likelihood that you can prevent that attack without advanced explicit intelligence is negligible. Some of the measures, controls and operational procedures listed in your threat level–based continuum may influence the potential terrorist action to take place at the perimeter of the property, thereby reducing personal injury or death and structural damage. Having examined the drastic security measures implemented at shopping centers in Israel, we understand that terrorists are fanatics who are rarely dissuaded or deterred; therefore, many of the procedures of your Crisis Readiness Plan should be aimed at minimizing personal injury or death.

13 | Emergency and Disaster Planning and Management

The *American Heritage Dictionary* defines an *emergency* as an unexpected situation or sudden occurrence of a serious or urgent nature that demands immediate action. A *disaster* is defined as an occurrence causing widespread destruction and distress. Most of us would prefer to put such events or occurrences far in the back of our mind, but the *reality* of managing a public-access facility like a shopping center, plaza, or community center in today's world tells us that we must plan ahead and prepare to manage crisis situations.

Traditional emergency and disaster planning and management considers events such as natural disasters, fire emergencies, workplace violence, medical emergencies and power failures. With the continuous flow of intelligence data concerning terrorist threats around the world, it is imperative that businesses and individuals prepare for the unexpected. In addition to the traditional forecasting and preparation, today's emergency and disaster plans should consider biological, chemical, nuclear, and bombing attacks. Clearly it is difficult at best to project or anticipate the delivery system for a radical terrorist attack; therefore, these attacks are virtually impossible to defend against. We can, however, develop appropriate responses aimed at minimizing casualties. In the following pages we will provide a blueprint to assist in the preparation of an Emergency and Disaster Management Manual.

In developing the Emergency and Disaster Management Manual, consideration should be given to a user-friendly, color-tabbed and numbered format separating each category of event (for example, Fire, Bomb Threat, Medical Emergency). Each section lists specific response steps applicable to that particular event. The listed responses are provided as a starting point and may not be all-inclusive.

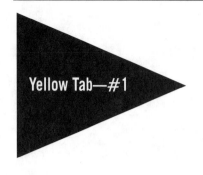

Yellow Tab—#1

CENTER EMERGENCY STAFF ORGANIZATION
EMERGENCY OPERATIONS CENTER
MEDIA RELATIONS

Each person predesignated as part of the Center Emergency Staff should be given specific duties and responsibilities tailored to the specific needs of the property and to each type of emergency event. Duties should be clearly defined and coordinated to assure effective response to each emergency as it occurs.

A suggested Center Emergency Staff may consist of the following, depending on the size and makeup of the center's staff:

➢ General Manager
➢ Emergency Management Director (typically the security director)
➢ Floor Wardens—number and description will vary according to each property

Common area monitors	Telephone monitors
Elevator monitors	Runners/messengers
Stairwell/service corridor monitors	Search monitors
Disabled assistance monitors	Retail tenant monitors

Since the General Manager is the lead person within the emergency staff, he should be kept informed of all occurrences on a timely basis. When an emergency is detected or identified, the General Manager should be informed immediately. The General Manager should advise the predesignated emergency staff members to assume operational command of the event by following the guidelines detailed in the appropriate tabbed section of the Emergency and Disaster Management Manual. The Emergency Management Director (EMD) should contact the appropriate responding agency, informing them of the details surrounding the emergency condition. The EMD should take operational command, provide direction to all members of the Facility Emergency Staff and remain in command until the arrival of the responding agency. The EMD should establish liaison with the responding unit commander and coordinate property emergency services as required.

A general listing of some duties and responsibilities that may be considered for the Center Emergency Staff (CES) follows:

EMERGENCY MANAGEMENT DIRECTOR

➤ Train and instruct CES team members
➤ Confirm detection and identification of the emergency—obtain details
➤ Notify appropriate responding agency
➤ Establish command post—normally security command center or management office
➤ Establish operation command with predesignated CES team members
➤ Communicate floor monitors appropriate to the event—provide direction
➤ Furnish current information to responding agency—continue liaison
➤ Provide emergency support as required/requested by responding agency
➤ Maintain current Emergency and Disaster Management Manual
➤ Insure center is maintained in a safe condition through regular safety inspections of all areas including tenant spaces—document hazards and remedies
➤ Maintain updated list of CES team members
➤ Identify and list all disabled or nonambulatory persons employed at the center (staff and tenant employees)
➤ Disseminate emergency response material to tenants and staff
➤ Conduct fire and evacuation drills as required by local code

FLOOR WARDENS

➤ Conduct or supervise emergency response training of subordinate monitors
➤ Understand appropriate response actions for assigned area
➤ In the event of evacuation, insure safe and complete evacuation of all persons in the assigned area
➤ Insure all evacuated persons go to a predesignated safe zone and do not reenter the building until clearance is received from the responding agency or the EMD

STAIRWELL/SERVICE CORRIDOR/COMMON AREA MONITORS—AS REQUIRED

➤ Monitor evacuation traffic in assigned area, insuring an orderly flow of traffic. Control access and organize the flow of persons into stairwells.

ELEVATOR MONITORS—AS REQUIRED

➤ Direct all passengers to the nearest evacuation corridor or stairwell and prevent further use of the elevator.

SEARCH MONITORS—AS REQUIRED

➤ Assist responding agency, *as requested*, in searching for unaccounted-for persons.

DISABLED ASSISTANCE MONITORS—AS REQUIRED

➤ Assist previously identified disabled persons in the event of evacuation.

RUNNERS/MESSENGERS—AS REQUIRED

➤ Provide communication throughout the center in the event of radio and telephone failure

TELEPHONE MONITORS—AS REQUIRED

➤ Handle telephone liaison between the command post, CES team members, tenants and responding agency

RETAIL TENANT MONITORS

➤ Each tenant, including theaters, restaurants, food court tenants, amusement centers and kiosks, are responsible for naming a member(s) of their staff as an emergency monitor. The person should attend emergency training sessions conducted by the EMD or designee. Tenant monitors are to familiarize store staff with emergency response procedures and cooperate with floor monitors in the event of an emergency. They should insure that the EMD is provided with updated information concerning the current tenant monitor and any disabled persons employed in the store.

➤ Anchors or department stores are responsible for developing emergency evacuation plans for their space. They should coordinate their plans with the EMD.

EMERGENCY OPERATIONS CENTER—"COMMAND POST"

The primary Emergency Operation Center (EOC) will, in all probability, be the security command center or the management office. The primary location should be used at all times when it is safe and has not been effected by the emergency event. The EOC should be manned by a radio dispatcher, the Emergency Management Director, and any other emergency staff members designated by the Director. Briefings, updates, and related operational meetings should be held in or near the EOC, preferably in a conference room or the management offices. All communications related to an emergency should originate from this location and be documented in an emergency incident log. Emergency-related communications should take precedence over any other radio or telephone traffic. Consideration should be given to equipping the EOC with the following *(If the security command center is used as the EOC, many of the listed equipment may already be in place):*

- Communications equipment—telephones, cellular or mobile phones, portable and console two-way radios, commercial radio capability, television, fax machine, megaphone system, elevator communication.
- A copy of the center's Emergency and Disaster Management Manual, site plans, building floor plans.
- A list of vendors and contractors who provide recovery services and materials—architects, plumbers, electricians, mechanical and fire sprinkler contractors, generator technicians, janitorial services, waste disposal services etc.
- Duplicate building security and fire life safety systems such as elevator keys, master keys, etc.
- Emergency generator capable of powering the EOC
- Emergency supplies or lists of emergency supply locations. Portable emergency lighting, handheld two-way radios, flashlights, batteries, safety gloves, bottled water, protective goggles, etc.
- Word processors, logs, notepads, tape recorders, cameras, CCTV monitor(s)

MEDIA RELATIONS

It is likely that an emergency at a shopping center, plaza or community center will draw the attention of the media. Understanding that, a mechanism should be set up to respond quickly and accurately. Releases to the media should come from *one* designated spokesperson who is fully informed and who has the necessary experience and expertise to deal with the media. Staff members and contract employees should be instructed not to discuss the situation with outsiders and to refer all inquiries to the designated spokesperson.

It is advisable for the center to adopt a position of openness as opposed to containment. In this manner, any release of information can be controlled and positioned to project the center in the most favorable light.

MEDIA RESPONSE PROCEDURE

1. Emergency occurs—detected, identified and verified
2. The Center's Emergency Staff reacts and reports to center's Emergency Management Director.

3. Predesignated Media Relations Representative establishes communication with Emergency Management Director.

4. As the emergency is contained, information is reduced to basic facts (for example, 2nd floor fire, east end, cause yet unknown, Fire Dept. responded, local evacuation effected, no injuries, business recovery plan being implemented)

The Media Relations Representative should discuss the facts with the Corporate Management and Corporate Counsel prior to a press release.

5. Upon approval, the Media Relations Representative calls a press conference—use five (5) keys:
   a. Conduct interview on your own terms.
   b. Create a central theme.
   c. Focus on what you are saying.
   d. Never lie, say "no comment" or go off the record.
   e. Practice presentation and rehearse material.

6. The Media Relations Representative should remain in contact with the Emergency Management Director for updates until the crisis has been eliminated.

7. Afford the media a final press conference/terminate the media event.

The following guidelines are provided for consideration of the designated Media Relations Representative:

- Preplan how the media will be handled—What type of information will be released?
  How can victims and families be shielded?
  How can we best protect our reputation?
- Will we permit photographs? Method/means
- Predesignated Media Relations Representative—should be management-level person for recognition/respect.
- Decide how the media will be accommodated—what kind of access will they have?
- Will we provide a staging area to keep them away from the event until we permit a controlled tour?

It's important to understand that the media will persist in getting a story that may not be factual and may put the property in a bad light. In dealing with the media in a controlled, professional manner, the nature and accuracy of information are more likely to be favorable.

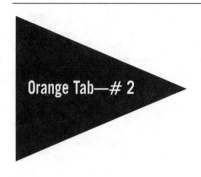

Orange Tab—# 2

EMERGENCY TELEPHONE LIST   **TELEPHONE NUMBER**

Fire   Fire Dept. [Fire Control]   **911** or _____

Police   **911** or _____

Medical
Emergency   Ambulance/County Dispatch   **911** or _____
Hospitals

                                Poison Control Center   _____

Chemical Spill   **911** or _____
Hazardous Materials— Chemical Spill Hotline   _____

Bombing/Explosion—Fire Dept., Police, Medical Responders (see above)

Bomb Threat   Bomb Squad   **911** or _____
                                ATF
                                Police (see above)   **911** or _____

Elevator/Escalator Emergency   _____

Electrician   _____

HVAC   _____

Locksmith _____

Plumber _____

Sewage Backup/Cleaning _____

Sprinkler System _____

Towing Service   Day _____

                        Night _____

Trash Removal _____

Utilities   911 or _____

Water _____

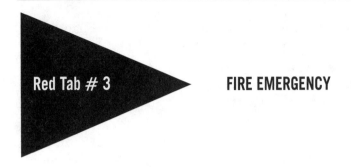

Red Tab # 3

FIRE EMERGENCY

In the event a fire is reported by a customer, tenant, or through the activation of the fire alarm system, the management office personnel or alarm monitoring station (security control center) should be instructed to immediately contact **911**, providing all available information regarding the nature and location of the fire. Communications should provide the following:

- Name of the center calling from telephone number _____ reporting a fire.
- Location of the fire—store, corridor, storage area, etc.
- The floor location of the fire
- Brief description of fire facts known at the time of the call.
- After the fire department has been called, Building Management, the Center Emergency Management Director, security, remaining staff, tenants, all customers and visitors should be notified. Vendors or contractors working on the property should be informed.
- Tenants in the area of the fire, adjacent, above and below should be alerted to evacuate employees and customers to a safe location.
- Fire First Responders should attempt to extinguish the fire using fire extinguishers or available water supply.
- The Center Emergency Management Director should assess the situation and commence evacuation as necessary; consider adjacent areas as well as critical areas above and below the effected area.
- A member of the security staff should be dispatched to meet the fire department as they come onto the property. Security should provide direction to the location of the fire.
- The Center Emergency Management Director should activate all or part of the Emergency Staff and implement necessary emergency procedures pending the

arrival of the fire department. Floor wardens and monitors should be activated as required to control the involved area. Search, rescue, and medical assistance should be called upon as necessary.

- Upon arrival of the fire department, the Center Emergency Management Director should liaison with the fire commander and effect transition of fire command. Assistance should be provided as requested by the fire department.

See Detailed Evacuation Plan For Complete Or Partial Implementation Breakdown By Floors And Zones

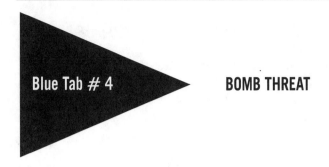

Blue Tab # 4

BOMB THREAT

Bomb threats are communicated in a number of ways; however, the majority of them are called in to the property. All bomb threats are to be considered real until complete evaluation of the threat indicates otherwise. While it should be understood that many bomb threats are made to disrupt normal business, certain logical and prudent steps must be taken prior to dismissing a threat as a prank.

Center staff, especially those at telephone switchboards, should be instructed on what to do and say if a bomb threat is received. A calm response to the caller may result in obtaining additional information. If the caller desires to avoid unnecessary injuries, he may be responsive if told that the shopping center is fully occupied with customers, tenants and employees and cannot be evacuated in time to avoid injury or death. It is possible that the caller may provide the bomb's location, components, or method of detonation or some portion of that information. Every effort should be made to calmly and systematically extract as much information as possible from the caller since he/she is the best source of information about the bomb.

WHEN RECEIVING A BOMB THREAT CALL—

- Remain calm—immediately refer to the bomb threat checklist.
- Keep the caller on the line as long as possible, asking him to repeat information as you attempt to write his words verbatim or activate a recording device.
- Ask for the location of the bomb and the scheduled time of detonation.
- Inform the caller that the building is full of people and cannot be evacuated in time—many innocent people will sustain serious injuries or death.
- Pay particular attention to background noises (motors running, music, etc.)
- Listen closely to the voice for identifying features (male or female), accent, speech impediment, etc.

- Attempt to alert management or security of a bomb threat as you have the caller on the line.
- Immediately notify management of the bomb threat after the caller hangs up.
- Management should instruct immediate notification of police, fire, ATF, local bomb removal squad (as appropriate)
- Remain available for interview by police.
- **Refer To Bomb Threat Checklist**—*complete form and hold for police*

Note: It is recommended that the main line coming into the switchboard be equipped with caller ID if available.

BOMB THREAT RESPONSE PLAN

- Upon notification of a bomb threat, the Emergency Management Director should assume command of the situation. A Command Center or EOC should be established, normally at the security control center or the management office. If the nature and location of the threat dictate, an alternate EOC may be established. In either case, the EOC should be set up in accordance with guidelines described in the "Emergency Operation Center" section of this manual.
- Building management should be informed of the bomb threat immediately after assuring the appropriate policing agency has been informed. The Emergency Management Director should analyze and evaluate the bomb threat using the following criteria:

BOMB THREAT EVALUATION CRITERIA

- Time of the threat
- How was the threat received (phone, mail)?
- How specific is the threat (type of bomb, place, time of detonation)
- Is there history with regard to threats? Does the caller or threat originate from a past or ongoing incident?
- Type of caller—a child, drunk, claim of terrorism, etc.
- Is it possible/probable that someone may have gained access to the claimed location of the bomb?
- After the initial threat assessment, maintenance, janitorial, housekeeping staff, and tenants, as applicable, should be alerted to begin a general search in their assigned areas for any unusual packages. Previously issued bomb search instructions should be followed. This is a **Level I** *general search*—based on unspecified information and the proposition that the bomb threat has little credibility.
- A **-Level II**—search based on more specific information provided in the bomb

threat entails designated personnel searching a defined area that is considered at peril. In this instance customers, tenants, employees and vendors should be asked to evacuate their respective locations in a calm, controlled manner beginning with the suspected area (floor) and including areas immediately above and below the suspected area. Special consideration should be given to the parking decks due to their vulnerability. Areas should be sealed off, and designated search teams should identify completed search areas with tape or a predetermined sign. As search areas are completed, they should be reported to the EOC for logging.

Note: Searches should be conducted by staff only when time is of the essence and the police or appropriate responding agency have not arrived on the property.

BOMB SEARCH COMMUNICATIONS

Traditional thinking requires that radio silence be maintained during bomb searches. Instructions dictate that radios and cellular phones be turned off. Modern thinking permits the use of two-way radios, theorizing that the bomber would not link a bomb detonation device to radio waves for fear of exposing himself to danger while carrying and placing the bomb. The use of communication equipment in a given situation is left to the discretion of *the Emergency Management Director or police commander on the scene.*

BOMB THREAT EVACUATION PROCEDURES

If a suspected bomb device is located through the Level I and/or Level II search procedures, the Emergency Management Director and the EOC should be immediately notified. A determination whether to completely or partially evacuate the center should be made. A security officer should be assigned to escort police, fire, and/or bomb removal team to the scene. Personnel should be assigned to remain in place, at a safe distance, to secure the area.

- Do not touch, move or otherwise disturb the suspected bomb. Do not attempt to cover the object.
- Establish a clear zone of at least 300 feet, including floors above and below.
- Open doors and windows in the area of the suspected bomb. Minimize primary and secondary fragmentation injury or damage.
- Evacuate the area as directed by the Emergency Management Director or scene commander.

Bomb threat evacuation should be conducted by zone or complete facility evacuation following a predetermined Evacuation Plan. Monitors should assist in the evacuation process in accordance with their prior designations.

In The Event Full Or Partial Evacuation Is Required—The Emergency Management Manager should:

- Determine if it is safe to use radios for communications related to evacuation.
- Begin the evacuation process by having messengers notify tenants and employees.
- Tenants should be asked to notify customers and employees in their space that a building emergency requires evacuation. Customers and employees should be given direction to remain calm, and directed to the route to the nearest evacuation corridor and/or stairwell.
- Monitors should be assigned to control ingress and egress to the building and parking facility.
- If a public address announcement is planned, insure that monitors are in place prior to the announcement. The announcement should be brief and to the point:

A building emergency requires that we evacuate the center.
You are not in any immediate danger.
Please walk to the nearest exit, where you will be assisted by a monitor.

BOMB THREAT CHECKLIST

Time of Call _____

Exact Words Of Caller _____

_____

_____

Questions To Ask—

1. When is the bomb going to explode? _____

2. Where is the bomb? _____

3. What does it look like? _____

4. What kind of bomb is it? _____

5. What will cause it to explode? _____

6. Did you place the bomb? _____

7. Why? _____

8. Where are you calling from? _____

9. What is your address? _____

10. What is your name? _____

Caller's voice—

calm	stressed	normal	squeaky	accent
excited	giggling	slow	nasal	disguised
angry	crying	rapid	lisp	slurred
sincere	loud	deep	stutter	broken

If the voice is familiar, who did it sound like? _____

Were there any background noises? Remarks:_____

_____

_____

Person Receiving Call _____

Telephone number at which call was received _____Date_____

Report call immediately to Director of Security

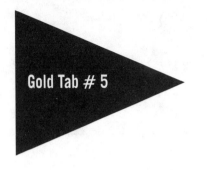

EVACUATION GUIDELINES FOR WARDENS AND MONITORS

Gold Tab # 5

The following set of guidelines is provided to assist zone wardens and monitors in evacuating persons from their respective assigned areas.

- Maintain calm.
- Encourage rapid response—avoid running.
- Avoid unnecessary noise. Listen for instructions from PA and other members of the emergency staff.
- Presence of dense smoke means—crawl. Use articles of clothing over the mouth and nose to aid in breathing; *do not wet the article.*
- Touch each door in front of evacuees to determine if fire may be beyond. If cool, proceed.
- Close doors behind people as you proceed. Do not lock them.
- Stop, drop, and roll if clothing catches on fire.
- If you encounter a smoke-filled stairwell, go to a secondary stairwell.
- Instruct ladies to remove high-heeled shoes.
- Use the stairwell handrail as a guide and proceed in single file as you descend.
- Avoid congregating in stairwell and emergency escape routes.
- Move quickly away from the building to a predesignated safe zone. Be cautious of falling glass.
- Dispel false information. Avoid using "fire" or "bomb." Use "emergency situation."

EVACUATION NOTICE

In instances where personal notification of partial or full evacuation is to be effected by messenger, the following message may be used:

EVACUATION NOTICE

A building emergency requires that we evacuate the area. No one is in immediate danger.

Please assist employees and customers to the nearest exit corridor and/or stairwell. Encourage calm.

All customers and employees should remain in an assembly area until an all-clear announcement is given.

Further information will be provided as we clear the situation. ***Do not*** call the management office or security—phones are required for emergency-related communications.

Security will contact you in the assembly area.
Be prepared to verify evacuation of your space and provide an accounting of your employees

The Name of the Center and Manager should appear here.

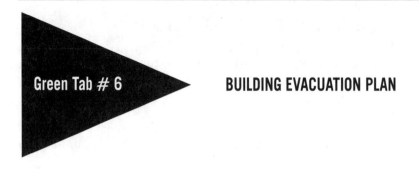

Green Tab # 6   BUILDING EVACUATION PLAN

The building evacuation plan should incorporate the use of security, maintenance, housekeeping, janitorial and office staff. It may be implemented as a total or partial evacuation at the discretion of the Emergency Management Director and the property's General Manager. The plan should be designed to work in cooperation with all tenants who are responsible for their respective areas. All members of the Center Emergency Staff including floor wardens, monitors, search and rescue personnel and tenant space monitors should work under the direction of the Emergency Management Director as the emergency event progresses. The nature and extent of the evacuation is completely at the direction of the EMD and the General Manager. Upon arrival of the appropriate responding agency, command of the situation is designed to shift to the commander of the responding agency. The EMD and General Manager should liaison with the emergency commander and provide support as required.

At this point in the manual a detailed evacuation plan should be spelled out. The property may be broken down into zones or grids with each area of responsibility identified by color, number, sector or tenant name. The plan should identify duties and responsibilities of each member of the Center Emergency Staff and how he or she will function in his or her assigned area relative to the overall evacuation plan.

A SAMPLE EVACUATION PLAN PAGE FOLLOWS
BLUE LEVEL
(level 2)

Blue Zone I—Extends from the south end [X Dept. Store] to the Flower Garden sector

Zone I Floor Warden—responsible for evacuation of the common area and all tenant spaces in an area reaching from the Flower Garden south to X Department Store. Insure that monitors in the area direct evacuation from the common area and in-line tenants to corridor **Blue "A"** leading to the garage and stairwells to the ground located in the northwest corner and middle of the garage. Tenant monitors should direct customers and employees to the nearest of the escape routes and coordinate evacuation efforts with common area monitors. Coordinate anchor store evacuation. Secure elevators during emergency status. Verify *All Clear* status with monitors.

Common Area Monitor—coordinate with retail tenant monitors to insure evacuation of customers and employees occurs through the nearest of the designated escape route, corridor **Blue "A"** leading to the garage and stairwells located at the northwest corner and middle leading to ground level. Report *All Clear* to Zone I Floor Warden and proceed to ground level by way of one of the designated evacuation routes. Act as a stairwell monitor as you exit.

Retail Tenant Monitors—tenants should direct patrons and employees to the nearest designated evacuation route, corridor **Blue "A"** leading to the garage and stairwells located at the northwest corner and middle descending to the ground level. Direct persons to follow instructions of monitors as they exit to the ground level from the stairwells. Coordinate evacuation efforts with the common area monitor, corridor monitors, and the floor warden.

Report *All Clear* to the Zone I Floor Warden and proceed to ground level by way of one of the designated escape routes. Act as a stairwell monitor as you exit.

Corridor Monitor-Blue "A"—position yourself at the head of your assigned corridor to provide direction to patrons and employees proceeding to the garage and the designated descending stairwells. Insure that there is no confusion in the corridor and that evacuation leads directly to the garage. Report *All Clear* to Zone I Floor Warden and proceed to ground level using stairwell. Act as a stairwell monitor as you exit.

Garage Monitor—Blue "A"—position yourself outside of assigned corridor to provide direction to patrons and employees proceeding to the northwest stairwell of the garage and down to the ground level. Insure that there is no confusion in the garage and that evacuation leads directly to the ground level. Report *All Clear* to Zone I Floor Warden and proceed to ground level using stairwell. Act as a stairwell monitor as you exit.

Floor Wardens and Monitors Roster   Latest Review

Date _____

Floor/Level	Floor Warden or Monitor	Post Assignment	Name	Staff or Store

Disabled or Nonambulatory Persons List

Floor/Level	Name	Store/Location	Nature of Disability

Black Tab # 7

MEDICAL EMERGENCIES
CHEMICAL/HAZARDOUS MATERIALS
EMERGENCY

Because of the number of people regularly occupying the Center (name) as employees, customers, visitors and vendors, it is likely that a medical emergency may occur at any time. These emergencies may range from choking to respiratory emergencies or seizures. Heart attacks are a more common occurrence with people operating under pressure or stress.

When anyone at the Center needs medical assistance, it should be communicated to the management and/or security so that 911 may be contacted. A medical emergency response procedure should be initiated in coordination with the 911 call.

Medical Emergency Call to 911 should include the following information:

- Building name and address
- Nearest cross street
- Level/floor of the emergency—specify where on the level (for example, 2nd floor at food court)
- Name of victim, if known—If unknown indicate sex, age, etc.
- Nature of medical emergency
- Victim's condition
- Provide call-back number at the management offices or the security command center

Identify the closest location for the medical emergency responders to arrive—inform them that a staff member will meet them

MEDICAL EMERGENCY RESPONSE PROCEDURE

- After calling 911, inform Security of the emergency
- Instruct Security Officer to remain with victim and communicate necessary updates by radio

- Detail a staff member to the nearest ground-level entrance to meet emergency responders
- Identify nearest elevator and a member of staff to control it through manual operation for a medical emergency
- If the emergency requires CPR, identify any staff members trained in CPR and direct them to the scene
- CPR should only be administered by trained personnel in critical situations
- If the center is equipped with an AED, a trained staff member should be dispatched to the location of the medical emergency with the AED
- Building management and the Security Manager should be advised of the situation in preparation of any media inquiries "see Media Relations" section (this manual)

A current list of CPR-trained employees should be maintained by the Security Manager

CHEMICAL/HAZARDOUS MATERIAL EMERGENCY

A hazardous substance or material is one that may cause injury or damage to people, property and/or the environment. It may be a gas, liquid or solid and may cause an explosion, flame, irritation, poison, radioactivity, or toxic effect. Any large spill or dispersement of a hazardous substance in or near the Center gives rise for some level of emergency action.

Any cleaning agent, lubricant, or other like substance routinely used on site should be identified with a Material Safety Data Sheet (MSDS) that provides the following information:

1. Product identification and emergency notification instructions
2. Hazardous ingredients list and exposure limits
3. Physical and chemical characteristics
4. Physical hazards and how to handle them
5. Reactivity data—what the product may react with and how volatile it may be
6. Health hazard information—how the product may enter the body, signs and symptoms, emergency first aid steps
7. Safe handling procedures

Products used in the following functions commonly performed at the property should be closely monitored:

Liquid offices supplies—cleaners, etc.

Maintenance supplies and materials—engine fluids, acids, thinners, solvents

Janitorial supplies—cleaning materials—cleaners, caustics, polishes, chlorine compounds

Renovation and construction materials such as paints and varnishes, sealants, asbestos, compressed gas

Note: Employees should be made aware that they must inform management of any hazardous material on or about the property. Management should inform employees who may come in contact with hazardous material of the MSDS Manual and how to interpret information contained on the MSDS label.

INTERIOR HAZARDOUS MATERIAL EVENT RESPONSE PROCEDURE

Procedures should be dictated largely by the nature and volume of the hazardous material event. Consideration should be given to the MSDS information as well as the location of the occurrence as it relates to customers, employees, and vendors.

➢ In the event of a Hazmat event, notify the Operations Officer and Security Director.
➢ Determine need for contacting an outside hazmat agency to address the situation.
➢ Identify which agency and/or call 911 for assistance.
  • Should the effected area be secured?
  • Should we control access?
  • Is it necessary to shut down HVAC?
  • Is it necessary to effect any degree of evacuation? Area? Floor? Section?
  • What postincident notifications are required?
  • Document the incident in a security report.

Note: Any staff cleanup work must be in compliance with OSHA regulations, and personnel must be monitored for exposure to health hazards during and after the cleanup.

EXTERIOR HAZARDOUS EVENT RESPONSE PROCEDURE

Procedures similar to those previously described will be largely determined by the nature and location of the occurrence and how it may effect persons at the Center.

➢ Is it necessary to evacuate all or any part of the building?
➢ In the event of evacuation, can customers, tenants, employees, and vendors use predetermined evacuation routes—stairways, elevators, service corridors?
➢ Can the HVAC system continue to operate?
➢ Is it necessary to seal building openings near the occurrence?

Chemical/hazardous material incidents require careful analysis with great consideration to the nature, volume, and location of the incident as it relates to persons in the immediate and secondary areas. No single plan can cover all possible contingencies. Respond to the questions above and formulate a plan specifically for the event.

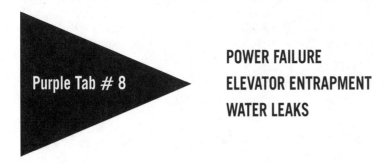

Purple Tab # 8

POWER FAILURE
ELEVATOR ENTRAPMENT
WATER LEAKS

POWER FAILURE

A complete (blackout) or partial (brownout) power failure resulting from weather or human error has a dramatic effect on operations at a shopping center. In either case it may be necessary to take some remedial action at the property. In addition to lighting concerns, elevators and all electrically driven machinery may be disabled. Computers and computer-operated equipment may be rendered inoperable. Equipment within tenant spaces and throughout the center may cease to operate.

Security or management should immediately contact 911 and **(local power company)** to advise of the power failure. Attempt to determine the cause of the failure and if power will be restored quickly. Determine if the outage is localized or communitywide.

POWER FAILURE RESPONSE ACTION

- Determine cause and expected duration of power outage from 911 and/or **(local power company)**
- Inform Chief Engineer/Operations Officer and Security Director—take further direction from them.
- At the direction of Chief Engineer/Operations Officer and Security Director, cause an appropriate announcement to be made to customers, visitors, or tenants—
- Sample Announcement: **(local power company)** has informed us that a failure in their system has resulted in a temporary loss of power to the Center. Please remain calm, power will be restored momentarily.
- Expected long-term power outages should dictate building evacuation or other remedial measures.
- Immediate attention should be directed to elevator failures and potential entrapments—see Elevator Entrapments & Malfunctions.

- Insure that restaurants patrons, tenants and customers remain calm within their respective spaces. Be sure that all customers and tenants are informed of the situation and respond accordingly.
- Confirm that emergency/standby lighting is operating throughout the facility.
- All computer systems should be shut down to avoid power surge damage when power is restored.
- Confirm that radio and telephone communication exists with fire and police departments.

Note: In the event total evacuation of the facility is required as a result of an extended power failure, refer to "Section 5—Evacuation Guidelines" in this chapter.

ELEVATOR MALFUNCTIONS AND ENTRAPMENTS

Historically elevators have been used as a safe means of vertical transportation. Modern elevator systems are equipped with numerous state-of-the-art safety features. State and local codes require periodic inspections and preventive maintenance to avoid elevator malfunctions and related emergencies; however, accidents may occur that require immediate and definitive response.

Some common malfunctions that may result in an elevator emergency response are:

1. elevator car not aligning with the floor
2. car stoppage between floors—occupant entrapped
3. elevator cars that "slip" during operation (cause improper floor alignment)
4. door jams—door not closing or opening

ELEVATOR EMERGENCY RESPONSE

- Contact Chief Engineer/Operations Officer and Security Manager
- Advise Elevator Service—800-_____
  —Inform them of the malfunction (type) and the exact location of the malfunctioning elevator
  —Request immediate on-scene assistance—determine their response time and advise the on-scene security guard/staff member
  —Provide details of the situation as communicated by security guard on the scene
  —Provide contact number for any return calls (reception desk)
- Communicate all available information to the on-scene security guard/staff member—insure that he/she remains at the scene of the malfunction/entrapment

- Establish and *maintain* continuous contact with persons in the malfunctioning elevator car
- **Instruct persons in the elevator car not to do anything other than instructed. Reassure them that knowledgeable help is on its way. Attempt to instill calm. Specifically warn them not to try to extricate themselves through emergency escape doors.**
- Constant communication will help passengers deal with the situation and help avoid panic.

Note: Removal of passengers from stalled elevators should be done only by qualified personnel.

WATER LEAKS

Water leaks may be caused by a broken or damaged pipe, sprinkler head, pipe freeze, blocked drain, overflowing toilet, or failure of a sump pump. When a leak is discovered, the first priority is to shut off the water supply to the effected area. *For safety reasons electricity to the effected area should be shut down prior to any cleanup of the area.*

A diagram of all major water shutoff valves should be maintained with this manual.

UPON NOTIFICATION OF A LEAK

- Identify the appropriate shutoff valve and direct it to be closed *if it is not exposed to an electrical hazard.*
- If electricals may be in the area of the leak or flooded area, direct that electricity to the area is shut down.
- Contact the Chief Engineer/Operations Officer, advising of the occurrence.
- Direct warning barriers to be set up in the area to prevent slips and falls.
- Post a guard or housekeeping employee in the area to direct customers around the wet or flooded area.
- Contact a plumbing service as required—see section 2 of this manual.

Maroon Tab # 9

WORKPLACE VIOLENCE
LABOR DISPUTES
HOSTAGE SITUATION

WORKPLACE VIOLENCE

The potential for a workplace violence incident at a shopping center, plaza or com-munity center is greater than at many independent freestanding businesses, since large retail complexes accommodate many customers, tenants and employees in one location. Statistics compiled by many sources indicate a continued rise in workplace violence in recent years. A number of authorities on workplace violence advocate a preventive action program undertaken by employers to minimize the possibility of a workplace violence incident.

Workplace violence incidents take many forms. Because of this, the following emergency procedures are general in nature and may require modification based on a given incident:

WORKPLACE VIOLENCE EMERGENCY RESPONSE

- Immediately notify 911, advising them of:
  the nature of the incident
  exact location of the occurrence
  number of subjects involved and weapon (if any) being used
  description of the subject(s)
  number and description of victim(s)—specify if hostages are being held and where
- Advise if medical assistance is required
- Identify the best entrance to use for access—inform them that a security guard/ staff member will meet the police there
- Provide the management office and/or security command center with a callback number

- Notify Security Director and Building Management
- Emergency Operation Center should be established (see section 1, this manual)
- Media Relations operations should be alerted
- Communicate with customers and tenants in the area, advising of the situation and suggesting they lock their spaces and take appropriate refuge
- Isolate the area—strategically post security guard/staff members at the perimeter, keeping the public out of harm's way
- Consider shutting down elevators and escalators to the area
- Consider locking service corridors, where possible
- Limit access to the entrance doors
- Limit access to identified parking areas
- Evacuate as dictated by the situation
- Identify an area for responding personnel to assemble
- Coordinate efforts with other security functions and police as they arrive—provide most up-to-date information
- Assist persons evacuating the site and direct them to a safe area

WORKPLACE VIOLENCE PREPLANNING EDUCATION

A number of studies suggest a broad general profile of the workplace violence perpetrator. He is described as a middle-aged white male who identifies closely with his job and is experiencing multiple personal or job-related issues. He may be identified exhibiting some or all of the following factors:

- a frustrated employee who has been through a number of jobs with little advancement
- a higher-level professional experiencing personal or workplace frustration—cannot handle job cutbacks or layoffs
- a totally negative person on life
- unable to accept personal blame for problems in his life
- displays a "short fuse" or uncontrollable rage over even the most simple situations
- a person with little or no support system to share his frustration
- someone who displays a propensity for or above-average interest in the use of firearms
- suffers from periods of depression and may be suicidal

Employees should be encouraged to advise the Security Manager of a potential workplace violence situation wherever and whenever possible. The workplace violence profile may be introduced to tenants as part of a tenant meeting.

LABOR DISPUTES, DEMONSTRATIONS, RIOTS AND CIVIL DISORDERS

Occurrences such as labor disputes can have a significant impact on the operations at a shopping center. Actions of the picketers may cause uneasiness among the customers, tenants, employees, and visitors to the property. Media coverage of such events has an adverse effect on the business. It should be remembered that private property owners have a right to secure and protect their property as well as limit access to persons to the property.

It is preferable to keep labor disputes peaceful and orderly. Persons involved in the dispute (picketers) should be encouraged to demonstrate outside property lines and avoid blocking ingress or egress to the property.

LABOR DISPUTE ACTIONS

- consult with legal counsel
- liaison with local law enforcement
- designate a member of staff, familiar with labor disputes, to assume overall management of the situation
- coordinate actions with Security Director
- Security Director should examine security requirements in light of the dispute
- post one guard at the site of the pickets—define their boundaries if on the property
- insure free and safe passage
- monitor and record activities—be prepare to photograph the site of activity
- inform customers and tenants of the nature of the dispute and of current actions—request that tenants report problems to building management
- keep media relations representative informed—provide periodic press releases (approved by counsel)
- instruct staff to remain neutral and minimize interaction with picketers

DEMONSTRATIONS

A demonstration is a gathering of people meant to gain attention for a cause. Normally such gatherings are not permitted on property unless authorization is granted by building management. Demonstrations that are not authorized should be directed off of the property. Security personnel should be instructed to monitor any demonstrations being conducted outside the immediate boundaries of the parking area to insure unimpeded ingress and egress from the property. Where necessary, the police department may be contacted for assistance.

Guidelines for Labor Disputes previously explained may be applied to Demonstrations.

RIOTS AND CIVIL DISORDER

Riots and Civil Disorders may take many forms and are prompted by a wide range of issues occurring in the community. Civil disobedience and the actions of rioters are difficult to predict. The following guidelines should be considered if a civil disturbance occurs on or near the shopping center property:

- the Emergency Management Director should be notified immediately
- Emergency Management Communications and Command Post with all of its components (this manual) should be established
- communications with the police department should be initiated
- photography should be used to monitor the situation and assist in strategic decisions
- customers and tenants should be advised of the situation outside the property— direct pedestrian and vehicle traffic away from the site of the disorder
- limit ingress and egress depending on the gravity of the situation
- Chief Engineer/Operations Officer should establish a standby team of maintenance and janitorial personnel
- the Media Relations representative should be kept advised of all actions and be prepared to provide information as necessary
- maintain a chronological log of all occurrences, deployments and actions

HOSTAGE/BARRICADE SITUATION

A Hostage and/or Barricade Situation may develop from any number of occurrences. Robberies, kidnappings, domestic disputes or workplace violence events may all carry over to a high-profile facility such as the shopping center. Hostage takers frequently are seeking public attention and use their action(s) to gain that recognition. Hostage and Barricade situations must be addressed on a case-by-case basis; however, all instances require the following:

HOSTAGE/BARRICADE ACTION

- immediately contact the police department, advising 911
  hostage/barricade situation in progress
  location, number of subjects, if subject(s) armed
  number of hostages, if injured
  descriptions of hostage(s) and subject(s)
  identify best entrance to the property to address the situation—post security guard/staff to meet them upon arrival

- set up Command Post/Emergency Operations Center
- evacuate area surrounding the situation—prevent customers and tenants from becoming involved in the situation
- isolate the situation
- utilize photography to monitor and strategize
- advise 911 to provide on-scene back up medical assistance
- alert Media Relations representative
- control and divert vehicular and customer traffic

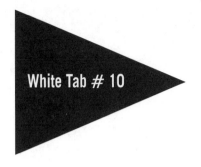

White Tab # 10

NATURAL DISASTERS—EARTHQUAKES
TORNADOES
HURRICANES
WINDSTORMS

Natural disasters encompassing tornadoes, hurricanes, earthquakes, severe winter storms and the like cause much property damage throughout the country each year. Additionally, people in the areas of these natural disasters suffer serious personal injury and death when not prepared to handle these emergencies. Some injuries are a direct result of panic when persons in a crowded area at the time of a natural disaster are not provided with proper direction. This section deals with controlling and providing guidance and direction during a natural emergency.

EARTHQUAKES

Although earthquakes are not a common occurrence in many parts of the country, some general guidelines for such an occurrence are provided herein:

- communicate to all staff that an earthquake has occurred—advise them to encourage calm in their assigned areas—guards should limit communications to emergency traffic only—report structural damage
- advise Emergency Management Director of the event
- initiate emergency procedures—evacuation, medical, elevator emergency, water leak, etc., (see appropriate section of this manual) as required
- customers should be encouraged not to rush for stairwells or elevators for immediate escape
- be alert for elevator entrapments (follow procedures for elevator emergencies—this manual)

- direct staff to keep guests and patrons from glass areas and hanging objects
- direct shutdown of all electrically operated machinery
- in the event of power failure, follow guidelines—this manual
- tenants should be prepared to go to emergency lighting—encourage customers to remain calm

Note: Be alert for an aftershock following the quake. Permit entry and exit only after structural damage assessment.

TORNADOES

Although tornadoes are much more prevalent in the south and southwestern parts of the United States, they can strike anywhere in the country and at any time. The spring months of April, May, and June pose the greatest threat.

A tornado is described as a violent storm, usually accompanied by strong winds and heavy rain. It is often preceded by hail. Tornadoes are identified by their characteristic funnel-shaped cloud. As tornadoes develop, they are commonly tracked by the National Weather Service, providing status reports consisting of:

Tornado watch—indicating the occurrence of a tornado in your area is possible
Tornado warning—tornadoes have been sighted in the area and are likely to occur in your area

National Weather Service advisories should be monitored by the building management team. Preparation for a tornado may include the following:

TORNADO PREPARATION

- alert Emergency Management Director and building management
- communicate "Tornado Warning or Watch" to security staff for dissemination throughout the property
- instruct maintenance to secure outdoor trash containers, portable signs and equipment or other objects. They may become flying objects in the storm.
- all doors should be closed
- restaurant operators should instruct all guests in the restaurant to move to an area less exposed to glass
- direct the shutdown/discontinuance of all nonessential activities
- office/store computers and other electrical equipment subject to power surges should be shut down

- customers and tenants should be encouraged to remain in the hallways away from potential flying glass
- consideration may be given to using the service corridors and stairwells as safe areas
- clear elevators and prohibit further use until all clear of storm warning

At the discretion and direction of the Emergency Management Director, in a critical situation, a Public Address Announcement may be given to encourage calm

- special notice should be given to tenants to prepare for emergency lighting-no immediate evacuation

HURRICANES

Characteristics of a hurricane are somewhat similar to a tornado in that they both bring forceful winds and heavy rains. Hurricane winds may approach 130 mph. Water damage from flooding, which often accompanies a hurricane, poses a great danger. Hurricanes are tracked regularly and with great accuracy by the National Weather Service. For this reason it is advisable to monitor news broadcasts. Advanced action can minimize personal injury and property damage.

HURRICANE PREPAREDNESS

- secure any containers or objects in the parking lot or outdoor area that may become flying objects in a strong wind
- move all water-sensitive equipment and merchandise to higher levels
- alert Chief Engineer/Operations Officer to establish stand-by crew in the event of power failure or flooding (see appropriate sections of this manual)
- lock off elevators at an upper level, safe from flooding
- shut down HVAC
- prepare for limited electrical shutdown
- close and secure all doors
- encourage restaurant patrons to move to the center of the facility away from potential flying glass
- food court and restaurant employees should be alerted to shut down cooking appliances
- prepare to respond to medical, elevator, and power outage emergencies (see appropriate section of this manual)

WINTER STORMS

Severe winter weather consisting of heavy snows, ice, freezing rain, sleet and hail may cause dangerous or emergency conditions. In many parts of the country severe weather does not dissuade people from venturing out to accomplish their business or pleasure. While there is no single emergency plan to accommodate all possible winter conditions, the following measures should be given attention:

WINTER STORM PREPAREDNESS

Monitor the National Weather Service for winter storm warnings.

- insure that areas of ingress and egress are clear of obstruction and safe to walk or drive on
- be prepared to address freezing pipes and flooding (see appropriate section of this manual)
- anticipate stalled or stuck vehicles—identify towing/car service vendors
- insure that snowplow vendor operates safely within or about the property
- insure that snow piles don't cause driving obstructions
- monitor building entrances for icing conditions and respond
- be alert to icing conditions on ledges above entrances
- prepare for power outages (see appropriate section of this manual)
- employees working in and about the parking deck(s) should be alert for medical emergencies
- record and monitor abandoned vehicles—conduct follow-up with police

EMERGENCY AND DISASTER MANAGEMENT TRAINING

In order to insure the effective implementation of the emergency and disaster management plan should it be needed, it is necessary to conduct training for center staff and tenants. Because of constant turnover of personnel within the mall staff and tenant employees, it is suggested that all or part of the following training outline be periodically reviewed with tenants and staff.

TRAINING OUTLINE
I.   Purpose of Emergency and Disaster Management
II.   Center Emergency Staff Organization
      A. General Duties and Responsibilities
III. The Evacuation Plan
IV.   Guidelines for Wardens and Monitors

V.   Zone and Sector Designations
     A. Orientation
     B. Identification of escape routes
VI.   Specific Duties and Responsibilities
VII. Special Assignments
VIII. Additional Tenant Responsibilities
     A. Notification of nonambulatory personnel
     B. Update "in-house" monitors—inform mall security
     C. Alert security of emergency occurrence
     D. Warn security of potential workplace violence situation

While there can be no cookie-cutter Emergency and Disaster Management plan or model suitable for all shopping centers, plazas or community centers, the foregoing is meant to serve as a guide to the development of a plan for your property.

14 | The Reality of Marketing A Shopping Center Security Program

Does it really make sense to market security? You can't touch, feel or smell security. There are expenses associated with marketing. Traditionally, when marketing places or things, there is an expectation of return on investment. Security is already an expense; how can we expect a return on investment for something that has no value and is already a drain on the income stream? How can we place a value on an inanimate service like security? If we highlight our security function, are we suggesting that our property is dangerous? Doesn't a security marketing program create additional liability exposure to our property? Aren't we promising total protection and safety to patrons, employees, vendors and tenants while on our property? Don't the risks of marketing security or our public safety function far outweigh the advantages? These are all typical questions and concerns voiced by many who have not taken the opportunity to analyze a number of factors.

The questions that are commonly raised regarding whether or not to market security fit into three (3) basic categories:

- Is there a value to the security function?
- Is there liability in marketing security?
- Is there a cost benefit in marketing security?

We'll attempt to answer these questions in a way that may help you decide whether marketing your security function may be worthwhile for your center.

Security has value
While it is often difficult to quantify what didn't happen because of successful detection, deterrence or risk management, it should be recognized that the operational success of security helps reduce or minimize personal injury accidents and claims as well as criminal occurrences at your center. In order to get a clearer picture of the value of security on your property, it may be helpful to require security man-

agement to document and schedule all safety hazards reported by security for correction. Clearly, if safety hazards are identified promptly and corrected on a timely basis, the probability of personal injury due to those hazards is reduced drastically—this function has value. Through an incident analysis process, security can demonstrate reduced repair costs associated with vandalism and other property damage—this, too, has measurable value. Reports of interdiction of criminal activity should be considered as having a real value. It is far more difficult to measure the value of successful deterrence; however, property crime statistics can be maintained and compared month by month and year against year. If the volume and nature of criminal activity are trending upward, it may be time to analyze the effectiveness of the security operation. If the same measure is trending downward, it may indicate that security is working effectively as a deterrent—this, too, has value.

As discussed previously, the security operation has value as customer service and public relations representatives, tenant relations personnel, and police liaison officers. Customer and tenant feedback provide a strong sense of worth in these areas. The *reality* is that security does have value.

A creative and well-designed marketing plan will not increase liability

It is common practice prior to launching any marketing plan to determine your target audience. In marketing shopping center security, the target audience is essentially preselected; the audience is customers, tenants, employees, vendors, police, fire and emergency service personnel who visit the center regularly.

Marketing programs typically emphasize the positive or beneficial aspects of the item, location or service that is being featured. Any plan to market security should follow the same pattern. Posters, pamphlets, audio or video should highlight the customer service and assistance practices of security officers. Customers may be reminded of the many other components of the security package at a shopping center, such as helpful directional and informational signage, well-lit and marked parking lots, staff communications, and partnership with local police, fire and emergency services. An example of a positive security marketing message may be:

The text below may be associated with a photo of uniformed security officers:

Welcome to SuperCenter USA. This photo is provided to insure easy recognition of our helpful security officers. Our officers are trained to assist you in finding a location on the property and obtain assistance if you are locked out of your car or you experience mechanical problems. They will help reunite lost children or groups of people. Our officers interact with local police, fire and emergency services to help provide a safe, secure environment. Don't hesitate to call on them.

Claims of security's ability to *totally* deter and detect *all* crime should be avoided. Local police agencies, with all of their vast resources, are unable to prevent *all* crime. By claiming that your security function will deter and detect *all* crime on the property, you are essentially assuring patrons, employees, and vendors of total safety. You are setting your own security operation up to fail.

Similarly, if the property is equipped with a CCTV system, there should be no claim that the *entire* property is under twenty-four (24)-hour surveillance. While you may have an extensive and sophisticated CCTV system located throughout the property, it is not advisable to suggest that everyone is under constant video surveillance everywhere on the property all of the time. No matter how complete your CCTV system may be, there are always technical and mechanical limitations that preclude *total* and *complete* video coverage. If and when an accident or incident occurs on the property, there will be demands for the video coverage of the event. If the camera system failed to capture the occurrence, you have placed yourself in a position of weakness as you attempt to defend your property and its safety and security operations.

While emphasizing the positive features of your overall security program, it is advisable to avoid claims that promise performance that exceeds what is humanly or technologically possible. Inferred assurances of *total* safety and security are sure to increase liability exposure for your center.

A successful marketing plan should incorporate the use of more than one medium. An important aspect of marketing security is through daily performance and appearance. Interaction with police, fire and emergency service organizations in the community is likely to recruit them as proponents of the security function. Security management should actively seek involvement with local safety and security organizations to increase exposure in the community.

Local police, fire, and emergency services commonly have community relations officers who offer a number of safety and security programs that their respective departments provide to groups and organizations. Arrangements can be made for each or all of these departments to come to your property to demonstrate their equipment and services. This will convey a message to your patrons of cooperation between your center and critical community services. Typically, police may offer child fingerprinting, firemen may display fire equipment and provide home fire safety literature and emergency services personnel may demonstrate CPR or other emergency response procedures. Property security may provide pamphlets with shopping center safety and security tips (site-specific).

Note: Events such as these are virtually cost-free and have a very favorable marketing effect.

Marketing security will produce a return on investment.

In discussing the value of a notable and effective security package at a shopping center, we acknowledged the difficulty in quantifying value from incidents and occurrences that didn't happen. Much the same is true in attempting to determine the REAL return on investment associated with marketing security at your center.

Some barometers commonly used to determine the success or failure of a marketing or advertising program may include:

- Sales
- Number of patrons
- Customer feedback
- Merchant feedback

Determining the value of any promotional program is not an exacting science, since a number of outside factors such as tenant mix, seasonal shopping patterns and economic conditions may influence the indicators.

Whether or not marketing the security function at your center was successful can be measured by the same barometers as any other marketing program. If sales and shopper numbers are up and customers and merchants communicate positive feedback, return on investment is favorable. Unquestionably, if customers feel safe and comfortable in the shopping environment provided by management, they are likely to spend longer periods of time at the center and return frequently. More customers, more shopping trips and more time at the center equate to higher sales numbers. *This is reality.*

Marketing a valuable security function in a creative, well-designed manner will, in all probability, result in a substantial return on investment.

15 | Crisis Communications

The following is a narrative of a real event that took place at a large multilevel regional shopping center somewhere in the Northeast several years ago. The true name of the center and identity of the police agencies involved are protected, since it serves no purpose to divulge that information.

It's a busy Friday evening in mid-November at SuperCenter USA. The mall staff, including customer service, housekeeping and security, are operating with a full complement of employees. The security staff is augmented by two (2) local police officers. The mall is crowded with customers moving about on each of its three (3) shopping levels.

Unknown to management, security or the local officers, a task force comprised of federal, state and local officers are engaged in an undercover operation with a number of drug dealers that has taken them into the center's expansive and busy parking lot. The lot is congested with vehicles, making it an ideal location for police undercover operations. The task force is preparing to effect a drug "buy—bust" (a drug purchase from the dealers followed by an immediate arrest). All members of the task force are armed and in plain clothes to avoid detection and to enable them to provide necessary backup for the undercover police operatives.

As the "buy-bust" unfolds, one of the drug dealers takes the "buy money" from an undercover operative and jumps from a vehicle running toward and into one of the busy entrances of SuperCenter. Officers immediately begin chasing the drug dealer with guns drawn, pushing patrons aside in hot pursuit of the criminal. As the armed officers enter the center, they are observed by the CCTV monitoring station in the security control room.

The dispatcher broadcasts a radio transmission to security officers and special detail police officers, reporting the observation of men running through the center with guns drawn, knocking customers aside as they go. When one of the local police officers (working at the mall) hears the transmission, he radios his police dispatcher to determine if undercover officers may be working in the area of SuperCenter. When the officer is unable to confirm any police activity known to his department, he begins to give chase . . . not knowing he is pursuing undercover police officers.

Fortunately, before the officers confront each other, and before any shots are fired, a mall tenant trips the drug dealer as he is making his getaway through the common area with the money. As the drug dealer falls, undercover officers immediately take control of the situation quickly, identifying themselves as police officers to everyone in the area.

In the end, the drug dealers are successfully apprehended, there are no serious injuries to customers or police, and no adverse publicity comes from this event.

This actual event is used as an example of the truly bizarre occurrences that may take place at a shopping center, plaza, or community center on any given day. This incident demonstrates the importance of many kinds of communications among groups and individuals with totally different goals and objectives. In dissecting and analyzing the communication failures in this simple incident, we find the following:

➤ Task force personnel failed to communicate with local police, property management and center security.
➤ Because of this failure, local police were unable to properly direct officers working at the center.
➤ Center security control communicated properly what was observed by CCTV monitors and initiated action.
➤ Because center management wasn't informed of the police activity in the parking lot, they were unable to alert (communicate with) the mall staff.
➤ Had the officers been successful in their "buy-bust" in the mall parking lot, it is likely that newspapers would have reported the arrest and where it occurred, thus sending a false or negative message to the public concerning drugs at the center.
➤ The operational goals and objectives of the police drug task force centered around criminal activity and protection of undercover officers, while mall security and staff were interested in maintaining a safe and secure environment for customers and employees.
➤ Property management is constantly aware of public image and strives to maintain a good reputation in the community. The effect that media coverage of a drug arrest in the shopping center parking lot may have on the center's business is not typically a part of police planning or postarrest reporting.

This real-life example demonstrates the value and importance of good communications in critical or crisis situations from an internal, operational, and media/public relations perspective.

Because today's shopping centers, plazas, and community centers are focal points in their communities, any crisis or extraordinary event is likely to gain a high level of media attention. It is with that basic understanding that we should approach crisis communication.

We have all experienced communication failures or breakdowns in our everyday lives. We all know the importance of effectively communicating with our family, friends and co-workers as we function in our personal and professional lives. *Effective communication* in a crisis at a high-profile property takes on a whole new meaning. Ineffective communications may negatively impact the safety and security of customers, employees and vendors at your property and/or could have harmful effects on the business.

CRISIS COMMUNICATIONS PLAN

As is discussed in the chapter "Emergency and Disaster Planning and Management," emergency situations or crises generally unfold quickly, leaving little time to formulate a logical responsive communications plan. While it may be impossible to anticipate all crises that may come about, a complete crisis communication plan may include all of the emergencies and disasters listed in the aforementioned chapter.

Many, if not all, crisis communication plans may have company policy and philosophy at the foundation. Apart from that single factor, crisis communications plans should give consideration to the audience you will be addressing. Clearly, different audiences have many different interests and concerns. If the crisis involves victims, family members of the victims are likely to seek information regarding the welfare of their relatives, while the media may be reporting on the cause of the event and the likelihood of a secondary crisis.

After having developed a list of potential crises and considering audiences that may require responses to each, it is advisable to establish the following elements:

➤ Identify a spokesperson. (It is best to funnel all information through *one* spokesperson prior to release.)
➤ Establish protocols for the spokesperson prior to the release of information.
  1. Spokesperson should obtain information from the operational person in charge of the crisis/emergency, typically the Emergency Management Director.
  2. The property General Manager should be informed of information communicated by the Emergency Management Director to the spokesperson.
  3. Company policy may require that any releases are reviewed by legal counsel and/or a corporate designee.

4. The spokesperson should have training and experience in dealing with the media and/or other audiences.

5. The spokesperson or property management staff should establish liaison with local media, police, fire and emergency services in advance of a crisis situation.

6. Consideration should be given to maintaining records of all information released that is associated with a crisis. If the information comes from, or is a part of, police or emergency services reports, the referenced reports should be maintained.

7. Preplan how the media will be handled: What type of information will be released? How can victims and families be shielded? How can we best protect our reputation?

8. Establish guidelines and procedures for providing access to the media.

9. Consider whether photographs will be permitted. Method/means.

10. Determine if a staging area for the media will be used to keep them away from the event until a controlled tour is permitted.

The crisis communication plan should be reviewed and updated periodically. Personnel involved with the implementation of the plan should be encouraged to create mock situations, discuss anticipated media questions, and train in accordance with the protocols contained in the crisis communications plan.

MEDIA RELATIONS

Because of the high likelihood that *any* crisis event or unusual occurrence that may unfold at a shopping center will become a newsworthy item, good relationships with the media are essential. Solid, trusting relationships with the media may be developed when deadlines and storylines are not at the forefront of a meeting or conversation. It is important that members of the media gain an understanding of the shopping center business and become familiar with local and regional management. The media should be introduced to the company's business philosophy in dealing with them. Initial "relationship" meetings should be aimed at developing needs and interests of the individual media representatives. Learn the types of stories and material that interest each media representative. Understand their deadline reporting requirements. Some of the key steps in a proactive media relations program may include:

➢ Identify media representatives and compile a comprehensive contact list including newspapers, television, radio

➤ Include names, departments, telephone and fax numbers, e-mail addresses
➤ Note deadline information, photo requirements, target audience

Note: Because of turnover of personnel and assignment changes, it is advisable to update the media contact list quarterly.

It is advantageous to the center and its reputation to develop media relations so that when a crisis situation or critical event occurs on the property, media representatives will reach out for the center's point person who is known and trusted by them.

PROVIDING THE NEWS

The following reminders may be valuable in maintaining favorable relations with the media as the center's spokesperson addresses the media:

➤ Disseminate news releases fairly and impartially.
➤ Respond to inquiries promptly (within guidelines and ability to provide accurate information). Meet deadlines where possible.
➤ Be accessible, honest and credible with the media representatives.
➤ Assure that the information reduces uncertainty and avoids confusion.
➤ Do not request prior approval from the media of a story before publication.
➤ *Nothing is ever* off the record.
➤ Be cooperative.
➤ Answer questions clearly, briefly and accurately.
➤ Avoid "No comment" responses.
➤ Interject and emphasize positive aspects of response or termination of the event.
➤ Provide written press releases where possible.

A prompt, accurate response to the media in a critical situation is sure to minimize the spread of rumors and false information. A spokesperson who conveys a calm, confident, and cooperative demeanor as he/she delivers a brief, accurate accounting of facts as known at the time is likely to reduce fear, uncertainty, and panic. This approach is likely to "hold" the media in a controlled condition as they await updates on the situation rather than striking out on their own to obtain further information. Promptly releasing all available *facts* is likely to minimize inaccurate leaks from unidentified sources and will probably diminish the occurrence of prolonged media coverage. If the incident or event is continuing or has not been completely contained, the time and place of a follow-up media briefing should be established. This practice encourages media representatives to await further verified details regarding the event rather than seeking further information on their own.

In responding to an incident, security officers are trained to determine the who, what, when and where, and possibly how, associated with the event. It can be expected that the media will request the same information. If the answers to these basic questions can be verified soon after a critical occurrence, where possible and practical, that information should be disseminated in the initial release. *Only confirmed information should be released.*

Note: The identification of accident or incident victims or other similar information may be withheld for privacy or police investigation reasons.

THE REALITY OF REPORTING A SECURITY INCIDENT

Because of the focus on security in today's world, whenever a premises security incident occurs at a public-access facility such as a mall, there will be a high level of media interest. Depending on the nature and severity of the incident, inquiry may come from local, regional and national media. If the incident involves injury or death to the victim(s), it should be anticipated that reporters may press for the identity of the victim(s) and full details surrounding the occurrence (see above note). Clearance for the release of any information associated with a crime that has been reported for police action should be obtained from the investigating agency. Initial press releases associated with a premises security incident may include the when, where and how in general terms. It is not advisable to include detailed information that may compromise an ongoing police investigation.

Example: *At approximately 8:45 PM Wednesday March 24, 2000, a lone subject armed with a knife confronted a middle-aged customer of SuperCenter USA in the parking garage and robbed her of $58.00 and a package of clothing.*

There is no necessity to add language such as—*This assault occurred in an area of the garage that is regularly patrolled by mall security.* Statements such as this will lead to many follow-up questions concerning details of the security function at the center. In the interest of compromising the center's security operations, specific information concerning such things as staffing, deployment, and other security measures should not be released. It is acceptable and advisable to openly discuss visible security controls in general terms.

Example: *SuperCenter USA employs a well-trained professional security officer force that regularly patrols the interior and exterior of the mall. Our lighted parking garage is access-controlled and equipped with emergency call boxes.*

Since any information provided to and reported by the media in conjunction with death or serious injury may later be produced in civil action against the mall, it is advisable to discuss press release information with counsel prior to any press conference.

An International Council of Shopping Centers book published in 1994 entitled *Shopping Centers and the Media—Crisis Communication* offers shopping center spokespersons the following suggestions that are still true today and that may be referenced when dealing with the media regarding facts associated with a security incident:

➢ **Be prepared** — Know your message objectives in advance and practice using them to answer questions that might be asked in an interview situation. Keep current on related issues, understanding that reporters may draw parallels between your center's situation and events that involve other centers or the retail industry in general. Be prepared to explain similarities and differences.

➢ **Control the content**—You can guide the interview by helping the reporter understand the subject and issues. Assume the reporter has little or no knowledge of the center or relevant issues. Avoid technical jargon. If the reporter is familiar with industry language, the audience may not be.

➢ **Keep answers concise** —Brief comments or sound bites are more likely to be remembered and accurately reported if they are brief and to the point.

➢ **Never fill the void**—Some reporters, deliberately use silence after the response to a question to create tension and get the subject to reveal more than was intended. Avoid feeling compelled to say more than is necessary to get the point across.

➢ **Answer every question**—"No comment" is never an acceptable answer, and can be a self-indictment. If you don't answer a question, someone else may. Be cooperative. If you can't answer a question, tell the reporter why. If you don't know the answer, offer to attempt to find out and get back to the reporter.

➢ **Watch your body language**—Be relaxed and open, physically as well as in demeanor. Be conscious of your facial expressions and avoid crossing your arms (this communicates lack of interest and/or defensiveness). Dress appropriately.

➢ **Don't be caught off guard**—Stick to the message throughout your encounter with reporters, including before and after the actual interview. Maintain a professional posture. Don't allow the reporter's friendly nature encourage you to speak off the record. Avoid jokes, small talk and hearsay.

➢ **Avoid contradiction**—Assume the reporter will take a no-holds-barred approach to the interview. Be prepared for criticism. Remember, you are not on trial. Your job is to educate and set the record straight. Remain cool and focus on communicating your message objectives.

➢ **Take your time**—Don't feel pressured to provide an instant response. Take time to think about the question and your answer. If you don't understand the question, ask the reporter to repeat it. Always complete one answer before moving on to the next question. Keep responses clear and concise; it will help you relax and speed the interview.

It is not uncommon for the media to request access to the site of a security incident. It should be kept in mind that police are generally in control of a crime scene or accident. Prior to permitting or arranging for controlled access to the scene of the incident, clearance should be obtained from the police. If and when police approval is obtained to access the area at and about the incident site, it is desirable to establish guidelines for such an inspection:

➤ Any access to the site should be controlled and accompanied by a designated representative of the center.
➤ Access should be limited by defined boundaries and within specified time limits.
➤ Access that hinders or impedes police investigation should be denied.
➤ Property management should reserve the right to control the location and content of any photographs or videotapes. (Management should be sensitive to the backdrop).

Note: Depending on the nature of the crisis incident or event, consideration may be given to providing the media with preselected and approved photos taken by management.

➤ Media interviews using the site of the incident as a background should be denied.

Clearly all of the above guidelines should be explained to the media in a cordial manner well in advance of any inspection.

Throughout any continuing incident or event, or at the conclusion of a situation that drew media interest and coverage, it is prudent to monitor reporting for accuracy and correct errors promptly as they are noted. Copies of all media coverage should be secured and preserved for future reference.

OPTIONAL METHODS FOR DEALING WITH THE MEDIA

To be sure, the nature and magnitude of any crisis event may dictate the method or means used to provide information to the media. No matter what method is elected, the initial message should convey the who, what, when and where, and if possible, the why or how. Painstaking efforts should be taken to insure that any and all information is completely accurate and correct and has been reviewed according to existing policy. If there is any question concerning details that may be known only to the police or investigating agency, they should be withheld pending approval by a representative of the investigating agency.

The basic methods of releasing information to the media include:

1. **written press release**
2. **media kit**
3. **press conference**

4. media interview (one-on-one)
5. advisory notice

A written press release may be used in an instance where a newsworthy incident or event has occurred on your property but has not yet come to the attention of the media. If you are confident that the media will be inquiring about the incident, it may be helpful to carefully structure a written press release that provides all of the verified information known at the time of the release. Since a press release is written in the style of a news story, a paragraph may be inserted into the release that contains positive information about your center, its makeup and location and the number of customers that visit the center annually.

A media kit differs from the written press release since it typically includes general background material about the center and its developer and/or manager.

Advisory notices are essentially concise communication alerts disseminated to media representatives advising them of the basic facts surrounding an incident with a notice of date, time and location of a planned press conference.

A press conference is an oral briefing provided by the center's spokesperson to a number of media representatives. Conferences may be a clear, concise recitation of the facts with no opportunity for follow-up questions by the media, or may include a limited question-and-answer session. A press conference is likely to include more detail than a written press release. The press conference should be held in a desirable conference location capable of accommodating numbers of people. If there is a continuing crisis situation such as a hostage event, a schedule should be established to keep the media informed of new information on a timely basis.

One-on-one interviews are likely to become more probative. For this reason, it may be helpful to the media representative and the center spokesperson for the media representative to provide an advance set of questions. Such an arrangement allows the spokesperson to be prepared with answers to questions that may require additional research.

Property management remembers that while it is important to communicate with the media in a crisis situation, it is essential that employees, tenants, customers, vendors and corporate offices are kept informed. In all probability, corporate policy should dictate the protocol for informing corporate offices of a crisis situation. Promptly communicating verified factual information to tenants, customers, employees and vendors helps to minimize fear and panic and reduces the likelihood of rumor and misinformation leaked to the media or the community at large. It is advisable to establish an internal communications protocol directing the designated spokesperson to generate a memorandum or statement of facts to be distributed to all tenants as soon as possible after the occurrence of a crisis situation. Tenants who are directly affected by the event should be informed first, followed by all others. Tenants should be encouraged to direct any inquiries they receive concerning the crisis event to the center's spokesperson, whose name should be reflected in the notice.

A crisis event at a shopping center may be anything from a fire to serious personal injury. It may be a structural failure, labor dispute or hostage situation. No matter the origin of the incident or event, internal and external communications should be preplanned to effectively control the situation as quickly as possible and minimize the effect on center operations and tenant business. Effective communications with police, fire department, tenants, customers, employees, vendors and the media are likely to accomplish the desired result quickly and with minimum damage to the center's reputation.

Note: A detailed plan for dealing with police, fire department, emergency services, employees and tenants is included within Chapter 13, "Emergency and Disaster Planning and Management."

16 | Risk Management

In the book Law For Non-Lawyers *published by the International Council of Shopping Centers, Donald P. Pipino and Mary T. Pipino provide a concise discussion of common legal questions related to insurance arising from various documents associated with the shopping center industry. What follows is a reprint of that discussion that appears in a chapter entitled "Insurance and Risk Management."*

THE THEORY OF INSURANCE

Ideally, insurance could be defined as a device for achieving certainty by combining a sufficient number of like exposures to make individual losses collectively predictable. Therefore, in order to operate properly, there must be a statistically sound database to determine the "chance of loss." As used in the preceding sentence, "chance of loss" is the mathematical statement of the likelihood of an occurrence. For example, in flipping a coin, the chance of a head coming up is one in two, or 50 percent. However, if the coin is flipped only once, the uncertainty of the outcome is 100 percent, while the chance of loss remains 50 percent.

At this point we must introduce the "law of large numbers," which simply states that the greater number of exposures to a given event, the closer actual results will match up to the statistically derived chance of loss. Using the coin-toss example, we can be sure that in a million flips of the coin, the number of heads will, in fact, be very close to 50 percent, which results in certainty versus uncertainty. Therefore, for the insurance concept to operate as ideally as possible, there should be:

1. A statistically sound database to produce a reliable chance of loss statement
2. A sufficient number of homogeneous exposure units to allow the law of large numbers to operate

3. The transfer of the risk along with a premium payment to an insurer, creating a pooling of interests

Even this very rudimentary description of the insurance concept will cause the reader to recall many examples of insurance contracts that were entered into without the elements listed above. For example, several years ago, National Football League owners bought insurance against players "striking." The outcome was disastrous because in addition to other factors, there was a lack of both a statistical base for determining chance of loss and a sufficiently large exposure base.

We ask the reader to merely carry forward the concept that insurance is a legitimate device to transfer risk from the individual entity into a pooling of interests and that it is accomplished by contract.

TYPES OF INSURANCE

Let us examine, in a very general way, the major categories of insurance that are commonly purchased. If we define loss as the unintentional parting with something of value, we can best categorize insurance by the losses it is intended to cover. A very fundamental division could be:

1. *Property insurance.* This is insurance in which the risk would be the loss to property from any number of occurrences, such as fire, windstorm, or earthquake, among numerous other perils. Insurance in this area is a two-party contract between the insurer and the insured, and any losses paid are paid directly to the insured entity and/or a third-party beneficiary, such as a mortgagee. In addition, rent insurance is available to replace the loss of rents during the period of reconstruction following an insured loss.
2. *Liability insurance.* This is any insurance contract whereby the insurer agrees to pay on behalf of the insured entity any sums for which the insured is legally liable. It is well to note that in liability insurance, we are introducing a third party, the alleged injured party who is seeking money damages from the insured. Therefore, losses are paid to a third party and not to the insured, as with property insurance.
3. *Life and health.* Although it will be of no concern in this chapter, it is necessary to point out that there is a huge portion of the insurance industry that deals with the risks of premature death, health, and disability. These are treated in both individual and group policies and require a completely separate discussion.

INSURANCE PRINCIPLES AFFECTING THE INSURANCE CONTRACT

There are certain principles that underlie the insurance contract. The most fundamental of these, from which all other principles derive, is the principle of indemnity. Very simply stated, the insured entity should be returned to the same position after a loss that it enjoyed before the loss—no better, no worse! A few of the many subordinate principles that derive from this fundamental principle are:

1. *Insurable interest.* The insured entity should be able to demonstrate how the occurrence of the loss adversely affects it. For example, if your house is destroyed by fire, what, if any, is someone else's insurable interest? What do they stand to lose? Do they hold a mortgage? Do they have a leasehold interest?
2. *Actual cash value.* Since the insured is not supposed to be in a better position, should the insured collect only enough to be in the same position? Although the answer is yes, many insurance policies provide an exception to this principle with replacement cost coverage. That is, they will replace a 20-year-old building with a new building if certain conditions are met.
3. *Subrogation.* If the insurance company pays you for the loss you sustained and that loss was caused by a negligent third party, you should not be able to collect again from that negligent party. Therefore, the insurance company that paid you is subrogated to your position to collect from that negligent party if they so choose.

These are some of the common principles that will occur in our subsequent discussions.

THE INSURANCE CONTRACT

The document that actually embodies the agreement between the insured and the insurer is, of course, the policy. The policy is a contract, and if we analyze it as we would any contract, it is not the mystery it sometimes appears to be at first glance. The policy can best be divided into six elements:

1. Declarations
2. Insuring agreements
3. Exclusions
4. Conditions
5. Definitions
6. Endorsements

Declarations are those individual statements that personalize the contract as to the specific insured entity. Declarations include the name or names of the insured entity, the locations of the subject of insurance, the dates the coverage takes effect, the description of the insured property, and all other information pertinent to the entity insured.

Insuring agreements are the insurer's statement of the scope of coverage being provided. For example, it may say, in the case of liability insurance, "To pay on behalf of the insured all amounts for which the insured is legally liable arising from the ownership and operation of the property described in the Declarations." In property insurance, such a statement might be, "To pay for any physical damage to the property described herein and not otherwise excluded."

The third element, *exclusions,* can best be described by using a pie chart concept. If the insuring agreements circumscribe the entire pie, the exclusions are the slices of the pie that the insurance company takes away. In the case of liability insurance, one of the slices always taken away is liability arising from any intentional act of the insured. In the case of property insurance, it would be loss resulting from "normal wear and tear."

Conditions are listed in the policy contract and can best be categorized as the duties required of the insured, especially in the event of loss. For example, the insured is required to furnish notice of loss to the insurer as soon as possible. Further, the insured is required to cooperate in furnishing appropriate records. Conditions are enumerated in the policy as duties of the insured.

The *definitions* section of the policy is very important. For example, if a liability policy does not include coverage for liability arising from the operation of an automobile, how is an "automobile" defined? Is a golf cart considered an automobile? Is a motorized bicycle considered an automobile? In addition, what is the definition of "insured"? Is it only the named insured? Does it include employees of the named insured while acting within the scope of their duties?

Finally, the insurance policy will usually contain a multitude of *endorsements.* These are addendums to the policy, and in many instances, they are the individual coverage enhancements that broaden the policy to suit the needs and wants of the particular insured. For example, we may wish to amend the policy condition requiring prompt notice of loss. If the insured is the owner/operator of several shopping malls scattered throughout the United States and is dependent on local mall personnel for notification of occurrences, an endorsement may be added to the policy stating, "It is agreed that the insured's duty to provide prompt notice of loss begins only when such notice is received at the home office of the insured." This is only one example, and there can literally be scores of endorsements added to any contract to enhance and broaden it on the insured's behalf. Here are lists of examples for both property and general liability:

GENERAL LIABILITY POLICY ENDORSEMENTS

1. *Broad named insured wording.* Provides a broad definition of who is insured and eliminates the need to add all named insureds that are owned by, subsidiaries of, or controlled by the first named insured.

2. *Notice of cancellation, material change, or nonrenewal.* Standard policies require an insurance company to provide 30 days' notice of cancellation, material change, or nonrenewal of a policy. The cancellation notice should always be amended to at least 90 days for the benefit of the insured.

3. *Broadened pollution endorsement.* The policy pollution exclusion is amended to provide coverage for pollution arising from hostile fire, explosion, and sudden and accidental pollution occurring on the insured's premises and includes pollution arising out of mechanical breakdown or equipment failure.

4. *Amended definition of bodily injury.* Endorsement amends the definition of bodily injury to include mental anguish, shock, humiliation, discrimination, and emotional distress.

5. *Blanket additional insured.* Provides automatic additional insured status to entities entitled to such status as required by an oral or written contract or agreement.

6. *Notice of occurrence.* States that the insurer cannot deny a claim based on late reporting as a result of an unintentional failure to report by the insured.

7. *Incidental medical malpractice.* Defined as bodily injury arising out of the rendering of or failure to render medical, dental, surgical, x-ray, or nursing, including the furnishing of food or beverage and the furnishing or dispensing of drugs, medical, dental, or surgical supplies or appliances. Coverage is limited to employees who are not physicians, dentists, nurses, or other medical practitioners.

8. *Per location aggregate.* Designates a separate general aggregate limit for each insured location.

9. *Coverage for injury to co-employees.* Removes the exclusion for bodily injury to a co-employee and provides coverage for bodily injury to a co-employee in the course of the co-employee's employment by the named insured.

10. *Undisclosed exposures.* Failure to disclose all exposures existing on the effective date of a policy will not be a reason by itself for the insurer to deny coverage.

PROPERTY COVERAGE POLICY ENDORSEMENTS

1. *Broad named insured wording.* Provides a broad definition of who is insured and eliminates the need to add all named insureds that are owned by, subsidiaries of, or controlled by the first named insured that have an insurable interest in the property.

2. *Special causes of loss.* Covers all risks of direct physical loss to the named property unless the policy expressly excludes the coverage. Normal exclusions are flood, earthquake, and losses due to nuclear reaction.

3. *Blanket policy.* Single policy protecting all buildings, improvements, and/or

property at one location. May also cover various properties or property contents at several locations. Typically provides 100 percent coverage of a loss or claim in relation to any one property.

4. *Replacement cost coverage.* Replacement cost of property without deduction for depreciation.

5. *Boiler and machinery coverage.* Policy covering sudden and accidental explosion of insured equipment. Also covers mechanical and electrical breakdown/failure of equipment.

6. *Building ordinance and law coverage.* This endorsement covers the cost to replace or repair the undamaged portion of a building that does not meet the ordinances or laws at the time of the loss.

7. *Agreed amount clause.* This clause states that the insurance company agrees that the values insured are adequate and that the co-insurance clause is waived.

8. *Earthquake.* Covers harm caused by earthquakes, landslides, and similar activities.

9. *Flood.* Covers harm caused by floods, surface water, tidal wave, tides and sewer or drain backup, or substratum water pressing on, pouring through, or permeating foundations, walls doors, and windows.

10. *Business income coverage.* Designed to provide protection for the firm's income statement. The purpose of this coverage is to replace the operating income of a business firm and its continuing exposures during the time the firm's operations are totally or partially interrupted. The coverage will also provide extra expense protection for the firm to operate temporarily while the premises are rebuilt or repaired.

11. *Rent insurance.* Designed to replace the loss of rents during reconstruction following an insured loss.

INSURANCE VIS-À-VIS LEASES

In this section, we will discuss the more commonly asked questions concerning the section of leases dealing with insurance. The most common areas of concern are:

1. Landlord's and/or tenant's requirements of each other regarding insurance to be carried by each

2. Requirements of either landlord or tenant to be named as additional insureds on each other's policies

3. Transfer of liability by either landlord or tenant to the other by "hold harmless" provisions

4. Appropriate use of waivers of subrogation

5. Assignment of responsibility for purchasing insurance in "net" leases

Landlord's and/or Tenant's Requirements of Each Other Regarding Insurance to be Carried by Each

There certainly is a legitimate reason for the landlord and/or the tenant to be mutually concerned about each other's insurance program. In the case of the landlord, the tenant's ability to maintain its financial viability for the term of the lease is of utmost concern for obvious reasons. Likewise, the tenant, who has made a substantial investment, is vitally interested in the landlord's ability to maintain a viable shopping center for the term of the lease.

To properly accomplish the mutual goals, care and consideration must be given to be sure that the lease contract language will properly work with the insurance contracts required. Requiring first-dollar flood and earthquake insurance, especially in certain geographic areas, creates an impossible task. Such insurance is simply not available! In addition, the lease should reflect the financial ability of either party to self-insure, either totally or partially, depending on the kind of insurance involved.

Caution must also be exercised in drafting the language that describes the evidence of such insurance being delivered to the other party. Language should be avoided that requires such things as "certified duplicate copies" of policies, since this could place an undue burden on the furnishing party.

We would recommend to the reader that there be an awareness of the need for individual treatment of each situation. Even though certain pro-forma language may be used as a starting point, there is a need for professional oversight by a qualified insurance broker.

Naming Additional Insureds

Although the insurance contract allows for the naming of additional insureds, we should be sure that such additional insureds have insurable interest. As respects lease agreements, be sure that when adding either tenant or landlord, respectively, the language restricts the "additional insured" status to claims arising from the named insured's ownership of the premises.

At this point, let us expand our discussion to documents other than leases for a moment. There appears to be a proliferation of the practice of adding additional insureds to liability policies carried by shopping center developers. The current thinking seems to be that, like chicken soup, even if it does not help, it cannot hurt. We would suggest that there could be cases where it could.

Let us review this process to see how outside entities gain "additional insured" status under your policy. In many instances, they are named quite innocently. For example, Smith & Associates, a shopping center development company, enters into a joint venture with Jones, Inc., another developer, to develop and operate Gateway Mall. Under the joint venture agreement, Jones is responsible for maintaining insurance on Gateway Mall. However, Smith's insurance broker, who is being cautious, has the joint venture entity added to Smith's major policy to protect Smith, just in case something goes wrong with Jones's policy or the limits are exhausted.

The joint venture then hires Johnson Management Company to operate the mall on Smith's and Jones's behalf. The management agreement calls for the joint venture to maintain liability insurance for all claims arising from the normal and customary operation of the mall. Johnson Management is also required to carry insurance for liability arising from Johnson's negligence beyond the scope of normal operations of the mall. Furthermore, the insurance required calls for each to be named as an additional insured on the other's policies.

Complicating matters even further, Smith, who was not required to furnish any insurance, but added the joint venture to his policy as a safety backup, is automatically providing coverage for Johnson Management because the standard wording in his policy extends to any real estate manager. In the final analysis, this very well intended scenario could have many negative repercussions. It is possible that each of the three insurers would refuse to act unless the other two contribute. Who is primary? Who is excess? Can these horrors be avoided?

In the case of Smith, who was not required to carry insurance for anyone else but wanted the benefit of its own policy as a backup, we suggest the following should be endorsed into its policy:

> *It is agreed that Gateway Mall, a joint venture comprised of Smith & Associates and Jones, Inc., is added as an insured, but only as respects the interest of Smith & Associates, and then only as excess insurance over any insurance carried by the joint venture agreement. It is further agreed that under no circumstances will this coverage insure to the benefit of any entity other than Smith & Associates.*

As for Johnson Management, gaining additional insured status under Smith's policy, we believe that insurance extended to real estate managers unilaterally by the insurance company can be limited by an endorsement reading:

> *It is agreed that any extension of the coverage provided by this policy to any other than those specifically designated as Insureds, shall be at the discretion of and subject to the approval of the Named Insured.*

Why do we suggest the above safeguards for Smith? First, premiums are determined by losses. Therefore, be sure that the losses to be paid under your policy are the losses you wanted covered when you purchased the insurance. Second, losses paid on behalf of others can deplete the limits available to you. Third, your policy may be written with substantial deductibles or self-insured retentions. If so, the extensions of coverage may create a financial obligation for you to pay for the liability of others out of your own pocket, to the extent that the payment is within the limits of your deductible or self-insured retention.

As respects property insurance, bear in mind that anyone you add to your policy as an "additional insured" could be involved in settling any loss you sustain. In addition, they will be named on any checks issued by your insurer for indemnity payments. Do you want that?

Regarding third-party beneficiaries, such as mortgagees, there is in fact a standard mortgagee clause that properly protects the rights and responsibilities of all interested parties.

Hold Harmless Provisions

There are very legitimate reasons for the transfer of liability to another, and the insurance industry recognizes this and provides coverage (with certain limitations) for the liability of another that you assume. For example, a tenant in a shopping mall expects the landlord to maintain the common area and provide adequate security. In such a situation, the tenant may require language in the lease that says, in effect, "The Landlord agrees to indemnify and save the Tenant harmless from any claims arising from the Landlord's failure to maintain the premises and provide security." The language used in this example is, of course, overly simplistic, but it suffices for the point we wish to make, which is that there is a legitimate reason for this transfer and assumption by the Landlord, and his insurance policy will respond under the contractual liability section.

Conversely, the landlord may require that the tenant hold the landlord harmless for certain claims arising from the tenant's operations. Again, the tenant's liability insurance will respond.

However, we would caution the reader in a few respects. Even though your liability insurance provides coverage for contractually assumed liability under a lease agreement, be sure that you are assuming only what you believe is proper and fair. First, your liability policies may contain large deductibles and/or self-insured retentions. That means that a large portion of what you are assuming may come directly from your pocket. In addition, be sure that the language provides relief for you if the party you are indemnifying causes or contributes to the liability that is created.

One final thought on this matter is that caution should be exercised by all parties to avoid wholesale and indiscriminate attempts to merely transfer legitimate responsibilities to each other without good reason or justification.

Waivers of Subrogation

Subrogation entitles the insurer, once it has paid a claim, to exercise its insured's rights of recovery against a negligent third party. However, such an action by the insurance company is frowned upon by insurance scholars because:

1. The insurance company has collected a premium that is adequate to pay the claim without exercising that right.
2. It can place the so-called third party in a position to respond without the benefit of insurance. This is because of exclusions in the liability insurance policy.

Therefore, the insurance industry grants permission to its insureds to waive this right. If properly structured, a waiver of subrogation in the lease prevents an insurer from pursuing recovery. However, the party granting the waiver of subrogation can still make a claim against the third-party tort feasor in the event the loss is uninsured.

An ideal waiver has three characteristics:

1. *Mutuality.* Each party waives its right of recovery against the other.
2. *Restricted to insured losses.* You should waive only on those losses covered by insurance—no waiver if you do not collect because of peril, deductible, policy violation, etc.
3. *Provisions for revocations.* Currently, the insurance industry permits waivers of subrogation without invalidating coverage. However, in case the insurance industry ever rescinds its permission for such waivers to exist, there should be an escape clause.

Suggested Wording for Insertion into Lease

The parties hereby waive all rights of recovery from each other for any loss or damage caused by their negligence, to the extent of the recovery under the insurance policies carried under the terms of this Lease. Either party may revoke said waiver if it is unable to obtain permission for such waiver of subrogation from its insurance carrier.

Net Leases

Frequently leases are entered into whereby the landlord wishes to transfer the cost of taxes and insurance to the tenant, thereby making the actual rental income "net." We mention this in this chapter for only one reason: For the benefit of both landlord and tenant, we strongly recommend that this be accomplished by requiring reimbursement to the landlord by the tenant of reasonable and proper insurance premiums.

Too often, we have seen clauses that require the tenant to carry such insurance on the landlord's behalf. From the tenant's standpoint, this may create an additional responsibility for the tenant of warranting the adequacy of the insurance furnished. From the landlord's standpoint, it is undesirable because in the event of loss, the landlord will be negotiating with an unfamiliar insurer.

Since the real goal is that of recovering insurance premiums paid by the landlord, simply state that the tenant will reimburse the landlord.

CONSTRUCTION AGREEMENTS

While a shopping center is being built, there are some special considerations concerning legal responsibilities and the appropriate insurance solutions.

First, regarding property insurance, there will be varying ownership interests. The first, of course, is the owner for whom the shopping center is being built. However, at various stages of construction, the contractor and various subcontractors will have temporary ownership of materials and/or partially completed phases. The insurance industry recognizes these special concerns along with the different problems created by a building under construction. Therefore, there is a particular policy contract, *builder's risk,* which is designed to combine the various entities and exposures under one policy.

Another area of special concern is the liability of all parties involved to the employees of the various entities involved in the construction. These exposures are included under workers' compensation (WC) insurance. WC differs from regular liability insurance in that it is a "no-fault" concept. The employee must only demonstrate his injury, with no allegation of negligence on his employer's part. The payment of the appropriate benefits is prescribed by the particular governmental or individual state laws. In addition, there is the general liability exposure to members of the public who may be injured and for which injury all of the parties—owner, contractor, and subcontractors—could be held liable.

The reader should be aware of the availability of an insurance contract that is designed to wrap up the exposures and legal relationships of all parties in one policy. Such a policy is referred to, as you might expect, as a "wrap-up."

One final comment on construction agreements should be made regarding the use of surety bonds. Surety bonds, although furnished by insurance companies, are really not insurance contracts. A bond or surety comes into existence when two parties enter into a contract, such as the owner agreeing to pay a contractor $50 million to construct a shopping center. The owner wants the assurance that the contractor will live up to his end of the agreement and requires the contractor to provide a responsible third-party *guarantor.* Such a guarantor or surety co-signs the contractor's responsibility to perform. Otherwise, the guarantor will pay the owner a certain specified penalty. That penalty could be as much as the full $50 million that the owner will have paid to the contractor. The reader can see that this is certainly not an insurance contract but rather a financial guarantee. When the occasion arises, a professional broker should be consulted.

JOINT OPERATING AGREEMENTS

There are some very special situations in the shopping center industry that present a very different set of legal problems vis-à-vis insurance. These situations are those in which the owner/developer creates a mall that has anchor stores that are owned by the occupant. These are usually department stores, and frequently such "operating partners" of the developer own not only the pad upon which their building sits but also a substantial portion of the parking lot common area.

The special problem that arises from these arrangements regarding insurance is the responsibility for injuries that occur in the common area. Usually a member of the public who is injured in a slip-and-fall has no idea who owns the parcel upon which it occurred. In addition, the responsibility for maintenance of the parcel might be other than the owner of the parcel. It is easy to see how a real nightmare could result from two or more insurance companies representing different entities trying to decide who is responsible.

Where such situations do exist, care should be given to align the insurance with the provisions contained in the Joint Operating Agreement. Frequently there will be a provision for joint liability insurance to be carried on the common areas. Unfortunately, the constraints of space in this chapter permit us only to call to the reader's attention the need for professional insurance assistance when such a situation exists.

SPECIAL ASPECTS OF THE INSURANCE CONTRACT

Before concluding, we would like to call to the reader's attention a few special legal aspects of insurance contracts.

First, although all contracts are contracts of good faith, the insurance contract is one of *utmost* good faith. The practical significance is that the insured has a responsibility to volunteer information that is material to the subject. Withholding information could abrogate the policy.

Another aspect of the insurance contract is that it is personal in nature. A policy of insurance covering a building owned by "A" cannot be freely transferred to "B" if the building is sold to "B." The insurance company must have the opportunity to accept or reject "B" as the new insured.

Finally, we must point out that the insurance contract is a contract of adhesion. The insured has little opportunity to negotiate the language contained in the policy. The significance of this is that the courts will usually rule any ambiguity in favor of the insured.

SUMMARY

We have attempted in this chapter to highlight some of the most common areas of inquiry posed by both lawyers and non-lawyers regarding insurance and its legal ramifications. By necessity, we have had to use a very broad-brush approach. We hope that we have succeeded in helping the reader develop an awareness of some of the most common areas of concern and the need to enlist professional assistance.

17 | Hybrid and Open-Air Centers

The International Council of Shopping Centers (ICSC) describes "open air centers" as properties that provide convenience shopping for day-to-day needs of consumers in the immediate neighborhood. Many of these centers are anchored by a supermarket and include a drugstore anchor. Open air centers are usually configured in a straight-line strip with no enclosed walkway or mall area and provide parking in front of the stores. Community centers, power centers, outlet centers and, to some degree, lifestyle centers fall within the general category of open air centers. The tenant makeup of these properties is the principle distinguishing factor.

Open canopies may connect storefronts, but an open-air center does not typically have enclosed walkways connecting stores. In addition to the straight-line configuration, open air centers may use an L-shaped, U-shaped, Z-shaped or cluster configuration. Lifestyle centers commonly use the cluster configuration and may have covered walkways provided for foot traffic between clusters of retailers.

ICSC describes a "hybrid center" as a property that combines elements of two or more of the main shopping center types. Common hybrids include value-oriented megamalls (combining mall, power center, and outlet elements), power-lifestyle center (combining power center and lifestyle center elements), and entertainment-retail centers (combining retail uses with megaplex movie theaters, theme restaurants, and other entertainment uses).

OPEN AIR CENTERS

The typical "footprint," structure and configuration of an open air center are likely to make it blend in with similar neighboring properties. Open parking areas servicing open air centers often permit access to and from adjacent properties. Plazas, strip centers and community centers are commonly designed with large open parking lots permitting customer and vehicle access at the front of the property with service and delivery areas located behind the retail stores. This property design with the associated customer movement and vehicle traffic patterns is likely to bring greater safety and security emphasis on the exterior. In establishing security requirements for an open air center, it is prudent to follow the blueprint discussed in Chapter 3, "Step One—The Study." After studying and considering the influencing factors including, but not limited to, location, tenant composition, building configuration, demographics and history of crime (volume and nature of crime), you will identify the property's security threats and vulnerabilities. Using this systematic approach you will discoverer *reality* at your property and you can proceed to develop a reasonable security plan that addresses potential security risks or threats.

While it is recognized that each property differs in its security requirements, a number of common issues may be considered at most open air retail properties:

➤ Perimeter visibility
➤ Perimeter fencing—definition
➤ Landscaping and shrubbery—planting and maintenance
➤ Property signage—directional and informational
➤ Parking lot lighting
➤ Exterior patrol requirements
➤ Delivery and service area controls and lighting
➤ Tenant liaison
➤ Local police, fire and emergency service liaison
➤ Emergency preparedness

PERIMETER

Assess whether or not visibility at or about the property perimeter is adequate. Topography, adjacent properties and local codes may impact the illumination and area of clear, open lines of sight that may be created; however, efforts should be made to reduce areas of dense vegetation at the perimeter in order to minimize potential areas of cover and concealment for would-be perpetrators.

PERIMETER FENCING

The value of fencing as a security measure at the perimeter of a property is often questioned, since most fencing can be easily defeated. There is little question, however, regarding the effect of fencing in defining property boundaries and establishing private property. If it is determined that fencing should be a part of the property's security package, lighting in the area of the fencing should be adequate enough to create a deterrence to trespassers and/or assaultive behavior at the perimeter of the property.

LANDSCAPING AND SHRUBBERY

Attractive plantings in and about parking areas and exterior courtyards enhance the beauty of a property and produce a welcoming effect for patrons. Accent plantings and landscapes should be regularly maintained. Overgrown shrubbery and trees on and about the property may create areas of concealment for would-be perpetrators. It is recommended to trim most bushy shrubbery not to exceed 42 inches in height and trees 6 feet from the ground. Consideration should be given to contracting with a local landscaping company to regularly maintain and trim property plantings.

PROPERTY SIGNAGE—DIRECTIONAL AND INFORMATIONAL

Since customers coming onto an open air center are less likely to come in contact with a security officer or representative of the property than at a traditional enclosed mall, directional and informational signage is important in establishing order and ease of movement on and about the property. Parking lot signage identifying zones (blue—2) assists patrons in locating vehicles after shopping. Security reminders posted on lampposts are often a worthwhile and proactive measure. Consideration may be given to prominent posting of property rules.

PARKING LOT LIGHTING

As discussed in prior chapters, parking lots at retail centers can be the scene of personal and property crimes. Since most criminals commit crimes where they *perceive* that they are least likely to be observed, it is important to install and maintain adequate lighting levels in parking lots. Open centers with courtyards and customer pathways should evaluate lighting in those areas to insure it is adequate.

EXTERIOR PATROL REQUIREMENTS

If, after a reasonable study, it is determined that a security officer presence should be a part of the overall security plan for the property, you will need to decide which of the following options listed in Chapter 4 are most suited to your needs:

➢ Dedicated security staff—Proprietary (full or part-time)
➢ Dedicated security staff—Contractor (full or part-time)
➢ Shared contract security—part-time
➢ Off-duty police officer—part-time
➢ Special arrangement with police or sheriff for periodic patrols (part-time)
➢ Police substation on property (full-time or part-time)

Chapter 4, "Reality—A Security Officer Requirement," provides guidance and direction regarding many issues associated with the selection, hiring, contracting, training, management, staffing, deployment and evaluation of security officers and contractors.

Chapter 10 discusses five (5) basic patrol techniques and the suggested application for each. Vehicle and bicycle patrol are most commonly used in the open environment retail environment. Mobile patrol techniques and management of that form of patrol are discussed in detail within chapter 10.

In the event it is decided to work with local police to establish the required exterior patrol, Chapter 6, "Partnering with Police, Fire and Emergency Services," provides advice regarding initiating a good working relationship with the police. This chapter also discusses common issues to be reviewed as well as the use and supervision of police at a center.

Consideration may be given to the creation of a police (fire and emergency services) substation on the property. Issues surrounding this arrangement may be reviewed in Chapter 6.

DELIVERY AND SERVICE AREA CONTROLS AND LIGHTING

The design of many open air centers often positions tenant loading docks adjacent to a service road at the rear of the stores. Since tenant deliveries may arrive in the evening or in the early morning hours when it may be dark or there is minimal traffic on the property and because, in many instances, loading docks are located away from the primary traffic flow, consideration may be given to assure that adequate lighting and/or access controls are in place at the service road area.

TENANT LIAISON

Much can be learned regarding virtually all aspects of property operations and activity from regular tenant visits. Recognizably, instances sometimes occur where off-site managers are not made aware of operational deficiencies or security issues that require prompt action. In response to that potential occurrence, a dedicated program aimed at good merchant relations and security awareness may be helpful to property management and tenants alike.

Tenant watch programs tailored after neighborhood watch programs may be effective in warning other merchants of patterned criminal behavior such as the use of fraudulent credit cards, bad checks, counterfeit money, organized shoplifting and similar crimes, but caution should be exercised to prevent against overzealous merchant communication and action that may result in the misidentification of a subject and/or potential improper detention.

LOCAL POLICE, FIRE AND EMERGENCY SERVICES LIAISON

There can be no question regarding a retail center's dependence on local police, fire and emergency services. For this reason it is important to attempt to create a good working relationship with these public services. A good partnership with municipal services typically results in a faster, more effective response from the requested department.

Suggestions and common issues discussed in Chapter 6—"Partnering with Police, Fire and Emergency Services," may be reviewed for assistance in maintaining and establishing relationships with local service agencies.

Because open air centers are commonly built among similar properties and are readily accessible from neighboring parcels and public roadways, they are more likely to be *perceived* as part of a retail neighborhood or district than their cousins, the enclosed mall. For this reason, it is often easier to encourage local police to patrol within the confines of the parking areas of open air centers.

EMERGENCY PREPAREDNESS

Regardless of the size and/or configuration of an open air center, an emergency and disaster management plan patterned after the plan described earlier in this book should be developed. While smaller plazas and/or strip centers may not require a complex plan, nonetheless, a plan specific to your property anticipating reasonably expected emergencies and disasters should be in place.

HYBRID CENTERS

Open courtyards, food courts and connecting walkways found in hybrid open air centers may be likened to common areas or public space in traditional enclosed shopping centers. As such, similar safety and security issues may be considered. The pattern of walkways and courtyards present at hybrid open air centers encourages large numbers of customers to traverse the property within these defined routes. If a security evaluation or study indicates the requirement for a security officer presence or the installation of security hardware, these areas of convergence and concentrated customer foot traffic should be considered. From a safety and security perspective, it is important that adequate lighting is in place along walkways.

Open air centers are designed to establish greater accessibility for customers. While greater accessibility may be better for business, it may create added security issues to be addressed. For this reason a number of CEPTED (crime prevention through environment control) strategies discussed in Chapter 3 should be considered for hybrid open air centers.

Small shopping plazas and strip centers located in communities across the country may function each day without an on-site property manager. Property owners and/or managers find it more economical to assign a single manager to multiple properties located in nearby communities, thus creating an absentee management situation. This arrangement is most effective when accompanied by a solid tenant relations program that stresses regular and consistent communications. A constant interchange of information regarding property operations and activity allows management to adjust and change operations, including security measures, on a timely basis.

Currently there is camera technology on the market that permits remote monitoring of multiple properties. Video signals from multiple properties can be transmitted to a central point or to selected monitoring stations operated by a contract service. This technology may be helpful in managing multiple properties but should not be used exclusive of all other security practices. It is not advisable to operate a camera system that is a) not physically monitored or b) not associated with a physical response, if required.

In determining appropriate site-specific security controls and measures for a hybrid center or an open air center, it is suggested that you follow guidelines outlined in Chapter 3, "Step One—The Study." After reaching reasonable conclusions regarding potential threats and/or risks, you may want to refer to previous chapters that discuss security officers and police as well as security equipment.

While many of the basic principles related to officers and security hardware apply universally, all security measures, controls, policies and procedures should always be tailored to the specific property.

18 | Real Incidents— Real Responses

Shopping centers, plazas, strip centers and community centers are designed to attract large numbers of people and to encourage the patrons to remain on the property for extended periods of time as they shop, eat and enjoy entertainment. Concert halls, stadiums, museums, retail centers and virtually all types of public-access facilities experience some level and type of safety and security issues and incidents on their respective properties. The size of the property, building configuration, tenant mix, and volume of traffic are a few of the factors that may influence the number and type of incidents that may be anticipated at a given center. The spectrum of incidents may include everything from slips, trips and falls to purse snatching. Shopping center management and security may have to address larceny, customer disputes and medical emergencies. Clearly every shoplifting incident, auto accident, and trespass encompasses a different set of circumstances. To create a "cookie cutter" set of responses to each type of incident is difficult at best. In this chapter we will provide a generic set of suggested responses for a number of occurrences that may be anticipated at shopping centers. Because the facts and circumstances of each incident vary, the suggested response steps may vary accordingly.

What follows is a listing of various sample incident types and suggested responses. This list is not intended to be all-inclusive of incidents or events that may occur at a shopping center. As explained above, the most appropriate and effective response(s) to a given incident may vary depending upon surrounding facts and circumstances. This listing of suggested responses is not meant to indicate that the responding officer or mall representative must address each incident with all of the suggested responses or proceed in the specific order as listed.

Aggravated Assault—an unlawful attack by one person upon another for the purpose of inflicting serious bodily injury.

SUGGESTED RESPONSES

➤ Upon notification or observation, notify command and control and supervisor requesting backup.

➤ Request police assistance if required.

➤ Attempt to verbally mediate the dispute, if possible. Separate parties.

➤ Attempt to determine which person is the aggressor.

➤ If one of the parties appears to be in jeopardy of or sustaining severe physical harm, initiate physical intervention—insure backup is available. Use only the force necessary to protect the victim and yourself.

➤ When situation is controlled and parties are separated, independently advise parties of their right to file a complaint with the police.

➤ Determine if injuries were sustained. Request Emergency Medical Services as necessary.

➤ Verify supervisor will notify center manager, upper-level management and legal as required by company policy.

➤ Complete incident report.

Barring Notice and Criminal Trespass—official notification of restricted access to the property based on inappropriate or criminal behavior (based on property rules). Violation of barring notice may result in notice of criminal trespass.

SUGGESTED RESPONSES

➤ Observe property rules violation or receive verified report of criminal violation on property.

➤ Conduct appropriate investigation to verify complaints that are not observed.

➤ Discuss repeated property rules violation with violators. Inform them of possible issuance of barring notice.

➤ Complete incident report.

➤ Discuss possible barring notice with supervisor or management as required by company policy.

➤ If barred person(s) appears on premises, remind them of restricted status and escort them from the property. If violator fails to comply, command and control should be notified with a request to call local police in response to a criminal trespass. Request supervisory assistance as required.

Shoplifting Assists—assist merchant or loss prevention officer regarding larceny of merchandise.

SUGGESTED RESPONSES

➤ Obtain name, address, employer and contact number for merchant witnesses or LP officer.

➤ Obtain details of the incident from merchant or LP. Determine complete description of perpetrator and stolen merchandise.

➤ Determine if tenant intends to sign a police complaint. Contact police as required.

➤ If prosecution will be sought, contact command and control with pertinent facts alerting dispatcher that shoplifting was observed by a merchant (or appropriate complainant). Caution officer not to make an arrest or detention. Request assistance in locating the suspect for merchant identification.

➤ Notify supervisor of situation.

➤ Insure that merchant and/or LP is aware that security officer(s) will not effect an arrest unless they observed the larceny.

➤ Stand by for police arrival and as support for merchant, as situation dictates.

Vandalism—malicious destruction or defacing of property.

SUGGESTED RESPONSES

➤ If in progress, notify supervisor of the nature of the act and its location; request backup.

➤ Attempt to detain where possible. Record identifying data, vehicle numbers and/or witness information.

➤ Contact police as situation dictates.

➤ Complete incident report.

Motor Vehicle Theft—theft or attempted theft of a motor vehicle

SUGGESTED RESPONSES

➤ Upon notification of lost or stolen vehicle, obtain complete vehicle descriptive data including make, model, year, license number (state), unique features, when and where vehicle was parked and by whom. Secure owner data—name, address, telephone number, circumstances surrounding theft (if known)

➤ Notify supervisor through command and control.

➤ Insure pertinent information is broadcast to exterior patrol units. Request property search for missing vehicle.

➤ Examine crime scene for evidence of breaking and entering of vehicle.

➤ Interview customers who may have observed persons near or about the stolen vehicle.
➤ Contact local police for response to motor vehicle theft.
➤ Complete incident report.

Medical Emergency—slip and fall, seizure, heart attack, etc.

SUGGESTED RESPONSES

➤ Immediately respond to the scene of reported emergency. Assess situation.
➤ Contact command and control and supervisor requesting emergency services, as appropriate. Designate closest point of entry to the event.
➤ Determine if medical professionals are in the immediate area.
➤ Apply appropriate first aid consistent with training if required.
➤ Keep area clear. Provide comfort to victim.
➤ Attempt to identify victim (through husband, wife, companion) as appropriate.
➤ Be prepared to pass information along to emergency medical personnel.
➤ Request backup as required. Insure someone is available to assist EMS at point of entry to point of incident.
➤ Complete incident report.

Purse snatching [robbery]—taking or attempting to take something of value from the custody of another by force or threat of violence and/or by putting a victim in fear.

SUGGESTED RESPONSES

➤ Promptly respond to the scene of the incident or to a designated location to meet with the victim. Determine if the victim is injured and in need of medical assistance. Respond accordingly.
➤ Notify command and control and supervisor.
➤ Obtain details of the robbery, including description of the subject(s), location of incident, method and means of escape, if weapon was displayed.
➤ Relay pertinent information to command and control for broadcast to security units. Request notification of local police. *If weapon was used, insure to use caution.*
➤ Attempt to identify and interview third-party witnesses (as situation permits).
➤ Search immediate area for purse or other items of evidence. Request other units conduct property search.
➤ Remain with victim. Insure proper transition of incident data to police.
➤ Complete incident report insuring appropriate management personnel are informed.

Burglary—unlawful entry of a structure to commit a felony or theft (forcible entry or without force)

SUGGESTED RESPONSES

Forced Entry
➤ Upon discovery, contact command and control and supervisor. Request backup.
➤ Request police service.
➤ Preserve crime scene. Do not enter area.
➤ If door/entry is to tenant space, insure tenant is notified
➤ If alarm is activated, call for backup and police. Do not enter space.
➤ If door/entry leads to center space, contact command and control, advise supervisor, and request police assistance. Preserve area and do not enter until police have arrived.

Nonforcible entry
➤ Upon discovery contact command and control, advise supervisor of unsecure door/entry, request backup.
➤ Enter unsecure area looking for signs of theft or vandalism.
➤ If no signs of theft or vandalism are present, secure the door and advise appropriate parties (tenant or center management).
➤ Complete incident report indicating action taken.

Larceny—unlawful taking or carrying away of property from another's possession or constructive possession.
➤ SUGGESTED RESPONSES (ASSUMING A LARCENY FROM A VEHICLE)

➤ Upon receipt of complaint, contact command and control and supervisor.
➤ Request that police be notified for response.
➤ Obtain details surrounding the incident, interview victim.
➤ Identify missing property, when discovered, when victim parked car. Locked?
➤ Remain with victim until police arrive. Assist police as required.
➤ Request command and control broadcast known information to alert other officers.
➤ Prepare incident report.

Clearly, security officers and members of the management team at most shopping centers, plazas, and community centers may have to address many additional types of incidents during the normal course of business. Events such as vehicle lockouts, identified safety hazards, automobile accidents, escort requests, and soliciting are likely to occur at any public access property. Personnel should be trained to address these and similar occurrences in accordance with management's business and customer service philosophy.

DEALING WITH TEENS

Dealing with teens in a shopping center setting, in fact at most public-access environments, seems to be a persistent and prevalent issue throughout the country. Some of the problem is a *perception* problem, since teens are often seen in groups and may be found acting out within that group to impress their peers. Groups of teens commonly meet at or near food courts, outside theaters, at or near amusement centers or at mall entrances/corridors. In many instances, small groups of teens meet and join other groups, resulting in groups or gatherings that become intimidating, particularly to female shoppers (possibly with a young child or children), because of their numbers and carefree teen behavior. Teen groups wearing similar clothing may be *perceived* to be members of a gang. This may or may not be true, but we all know that *perception* is *reality*.

Whether the teen problem is *real* or *perceived,* it is likely that management may have to address it through security.

SUGGESTED RESPONSES

➤ Establish a program that regularly and consistently identifies and removes truants from the property.
➤ As groups of teens are observed on the property or within the common area, observe their dress and behavior [physically or with camera(s)] to insure they are not gangs or unruly groups. If/when disruptive behavior is observed, require that the responsible individuals leave the property.
➤ If teen groups become so large that they impede normal foot traffic, require that they break up into smaller groups. If the group(s) refuse to comply or continue to loiter or become disruptive, require that they leave the property.

Note: A well-behaved group of seven (7) teens may not require disbursement, while a rowdy group of five (5) teens may require separation. It is very difficult to set an arbitrary number of teens that should be permitted to move about the property as one group.

➤ Establish a strict policy—"zero tolerance"—concerning fights on the property. Anyone guilty of fighting on property may be banned for a minimum of six (6) months.
➤ Insure that property rules addressing loitering, disruptive behavior, use of food

court tables, and unacceptable language are prominently posted at or near areas known to attract teens.
➤ Encourage security officers to be firm but fair in dealing with teens.

PARENTAL ESCORT PROGRAM

Upon determining that teen behavior was affecting business at their centers, a number of shopping center owners and managers across the country instituted parental escort policies that require persons under a specific age (typically 15 or 16) to be escorted by an adult (21 or older) on Friday and Saturday evenings. Parental escort programs require intense prior planning and community outreach and education in order to be successful.

An outline of some basic steps that may be taken when considering a Parental Escort Program includes:

➤ Research and Planning
    Review incident report—teen banning
    Tenant concerns/surveys
    Shopper concerns/surveys
    Review practices and results of other PEPs
    Evaluate results
    Consider budgetary impact
    Define specifics of the plan
➤ Public Relations Segment—must be timed properly
    Prepare PR package outlining highlights of PEP and why it is necessary
    Identify groups to be targeted
    Community groups
        Schools
        Churches
        Key political figures/community leaders
        Police
        Store managers
        ACLU
➤ Marketing the PEP—after decision to implement/prior to or in conjunction with
    implementation of the program
        merchant meetings
        employee meetings
        press releases and conferences
        advertising piece
        meet with outside organizations (listed above)

➤ Enforcement of the program

    Security Officer training—specific policy and procedures

        Age verification process

        Entry refusal

        Handling underaged without transportation

    Police officer support

➤ Follow-up review

While these policies and programs typically meet with early resistance from a small portion of the shopping public, they appear to have been very successful in many locations in the long run.

There can be no question that *real incidents* require *real responses* in order to maintain structure, order and public confidence in the shopping center environment.

19 | The Reality of Your Security Operation— A Security Audit

The term "audit" carries with it the *perception* of a critical analysis of records and accounts for purposes of uncovering illegal or improper accounting of money or material. This *perception* could not be further from the truth. A security audit is meant to review, analyze and evaluate existing security polices, practices, procedures, measures and controls and related operations to insure they are reasonable to address identified risks and threats.

In order for a security audit or evaluation to be valuable and effective, the entity being audited should adopt the notion that an audit will make security operations better. If upper-level management *perceives* that security has a significant value in the framework and objectives of center operations, periodic audits are likely to be welcomed and considered nonthreatening. The *reality* of security operations and their effectiveness at your center, under current conditions, along with suggestions and recommendations, should be included in the report of findings associated with the security audit. Recommendations should be prioritized commensurate to their relative level of importance in the overall security plan.

Periodic security audits may be conducted by an internal audit team or through the use of an outside security management consultant. In either case, the security auditor's goals and objectives should include, but may not be limited to:

1. Identification of physical assets that require protection.
2. Understanding personal security requirements.
3. Considering legal liabilities associated with the property.
4. Attempting to quantify security spending vs. potential loss of income from failed security.

Auditor(s) may accomplish these goals and objectives through a complete study and evaluation of:

➢ The property (location, size, configuration, tenant makeup, parking)
➢ Operations (management, maintenance, housekeeping, marketing, security)
➢ Policies and procedures
➢ Activities
➢ Security philosophy
➢ Crime history
➢ Social environment—demographics
➢ Community (involvement & influences)

Prior to the commencement of a security audit it is necessary to gather and record general information about the center. This information may include:

1. Date the audit was begun (and completed)
2. Name of the center (address & telephone number)
3. Property owner & manager
4. Organizational chart (names, titles, responsibilities)
5. Tenant list (type of business)
6. Emergency telephone numbers
7. Normal hours of operation
8. Number and name of tenants with extended hours of operation
9. Who performs maintenance, housekeeping, security
10. Crime history at property—past 3 years
11. Specific security problems or issues
12. Site plan or map

The following is a suggested outline that may be used as a guide in conducting a security audit. This outline is meant as a guide to understanding that factors such as size, location, configuration, and socioeconomic influences may impact the form and content of a security audit.

SECURITY AUDIT MODEL

LOCATION OF THE PROPERTY

- relative to an urban area
- major roadways/highways impacting the center
- proximity to major facilities—colleges, hotel area, retail district, area attraction(s)
- principal industry/employer
- local travel—public transportation to the mall

NATURE AND USE OF THE PROPERTY

- when built—renovations, additions, expansions
- total acreage including outparcels
- gross building area
- GLA—percent leased
- parking acreage—number of spaces
  access
  paid parking (?)
  parking deck or multilevel parking
  enclosed stairways
- building configuration (footprint) map
- sample store directory—identify anchors, identify tenants and services
- Is there a
  1. food court
  2. theater(s)
  3. amusement center(s)
  4. restaurant/tavern(s)—after hours (?)
  5. bank(s)
  6. ATM(s)
  7. hotels
- specialty tenants
- youth-oriented tenants
- special events hosted by the mall
- patrons per week/month/year—annual sales
- car counters or estimates
- tenants providing own security/loss prevention

DEMOGRAPHICS

- population profile
  principal employers, % unemployment
  level of education
  median income
  % home owners
  % male/female
  local issues
  ethnic diversity (customers)
- marketing information re: trade area
- local colleges and universities impacting the mall
- population concentration

SECURITY DEPT. MANAGEMENT & PLANNING

- Current hours of service (sample weekly schedule, deployment schedule)
- Identify Patrol Beats & coverage
- Security Policies & Procedures Manual   Updated _____
- Performance evaluations—frequency—criteria
  personnel files—contents
- Training—basis—ongoing—specialized—records maintained
- State certification (?)—compliance
- Officer appearance—visibility/uniforms
- Post orders
- Patrol methods and practices—
  foot
  bicycle
  stationary post(s)
  vehicle
- Vehicle Patrol practices—
  emergency light—activated (?) percent of time
  communications
- How are lighting surveys done—frequency
- Policy re: lockouts—jump starts—escort services
- Policy re: courier services on property
- Overnight parking reports—procedures
- Police patrols
  hired (?)—instructions
  substation (?)
  liaison—how (?) frequency documented (?)
- Fire Dept. liaison
- Emergency services liaison
- Mall rules published—how—where (sample)
- Communications
  equipment
  methods
- Policy re: interaction with tenant LPs
- Any bank escort services provided
- Identify electronics and technical support
  access control
  guard tour system
  CCTV
  motion sensors

computerized incident reporting
system of tracking and trending frequency
review with management

- Key control system
- Disaster & Emergency Management Plan—
Evacuation Plan last updated _____
- Crime Prevention Program
- Potential Litigation files
- Safety Committee
management of claims/risk procedures
- Samples of
  1. daily log(s)
  2. officer's log
  3. patrol vehicle log
  4. vehicle inspection report
  5. incident report
  6. recap sheet for incidents at mall (past 3 years)

SAFETY INSPECTION

- Emergency Management Plan
where kept
updated(?)
training
drills
- Fire drills
fire extinguisher inspections
- Emergency Power Generator yes/no
where
- Trash compactors
how many
where
access
method of activation
safety cutoff
contracted
- Inspect
parking lot markings
lighting
lighting surveys

crosswalks
signage
parking lot surface
curbing
landscaping & foliage
traffic flow patterns
elevators
exterior doors (locking)
loading docks
barriers (fences, gates, walls, etc.)
alarms—smoke, water flow, exit doors, etc.

CRIME STUDY

➤ Police calls for service to the property—past 3 years
   Meet with police "point person" or ranking officer and beat officer(s)
   Average response time
   Patrol practices at the property
   Arrangements re: use of police to augment center security
   Review beat or zone crime stats if available
   Evaluate relations
   Discuss special concerns
   Discuss traffic, special events
   Compare to nearby similar properties
➤ Review and analyze property incident reports—volume and nature of crime
➤ Emergency Services—Fire and Ambulance
   Meet with chief of each service
   Determine average response time
   Calls for service to the property—volume and nature
   Discuss special concerns
   Evaluate relationship property security

It is advisable to have safety and security audits done under supervision of in-house or retained counsel. The written report of findings associated with the safety and security audit should be designated as ***Attorney work product prepared in anticipation of litigation and limited in copy and distribution.***

20 | Selecting and Using a Qualified Security Consultant

It can be expected, particularly in today's society, when a developer is presenting his or her project to a municipal board that many questions will be asked about the kinds of security concerns the shopping center, plaza or community center is likely to bring to the neighborhood and the community at large. What impact will the project have on police, fire and emergency services in the community? What kinds of incidents may be expected at the property? Do you have projections? Based on what data? If the developer cannot provide reasonable answers based on a proper study of the proposed development, he or she may experience resistance and/or difficulty in obtaining necessary approvals to move forward with the project.

The *perception* that *all* retail centers are likely to create a high volume of serious security issues is common. The *reality* is that this *perception* and the associated attitudes may be just the beginning of unnecessary but consistent scrutiny and/or criticism of security at the property.

In order to present yourself and your project to the community in the most favorable light, it is prudent to enlist the assistance of in-house security professionals or a reputable security consultant during the early stages of your project. A prompt, conscious decision to outsource security may establish credibility, save security dollars, and avoid future headaches.

Clearly, the use of a security consultant(s) may be considered during the developmental stages of a shopping center, plaza or community center; however, they may also be valuable after the center is up and running.

If you do not have the necessary resources within your company, or you determine that an independent third party may add additional credibility to your presentation, you may require a security consultant. The search and selection of an independent security consultant should include a few basic steps:

1. Identify consultants who have worked with and have demonstrated knowledge of shopping center security.
2. Require the prospective consultant to provide a curriculum vitae detailing education, professional affiliations, and prior experience—at a minimum.
3. Request references—attempt to develop additional references as you interview those provided by the candidate.
4. Insure the consultant is *independent* and does not represent a security product or service.
5. Personally interview the candidate to evaluate his industry-specific knowledge and expertise.
6. Ask for samples of his work product or his model for accomplishing your objectives.
7. Evaluate his communication skills and insure he/she would be a good fit with your staff.

You will have to determine if your project requires a written RFP (request for proposal) that spells out the goals of the project or if you would rather interview a select few candidates and explain your goals and how he/she would propose to approach the assignment.

During the selection process, be sure to determine the consultant's billing practices. Determine his hourly rate and, if appropriate, request an estimated project cost and a "not to exceed" cost. Clarify when his billing begins. Some consultants begin billing clients when they leave their office (portal to portal). It is standard practice for consultants to bill clients reasonable expenses associated with travel. If you are interested in using the consultant on a long-term or continuing basis, you may want to discuss a monthly or quarterly retainer agreement that specifies a number of consulting hours for a defined period.

Keep in mind that security consultants may be used in many ways. Some of the ways that a security consultant may be helpful to developers and managers of retail environments include:

➢ Assist in the initial Threat Assessment, Risk Analysis and Vulnerability of a new property.
➢ Development of a security plan for a new property—based on results from the appropriate study.
➢ Conduct security audit or evaluation of an existing property. Report findings with prioritized recommendations.
➢ Provide security management and support where a security professional is not part of the "in-house" corporate infrastructure.
➢ Validate security procedures and practices (operations) as an independent, third-party auditor.

➤ Study critical issues and develop responsive, reasonable, and cost-effective measures and controls.

➤ Conduct review and analysis of fact, circumstances, and security practices associated with liability litigation emanating from a premises security lawsuit.

If you identify a need for a security consultant, it is paramount that you designate a representative of upper-level management familiar with your company's philosophy and procedure and with sufficient authority to insure that the consultant has the necessary cooperation to successfully accomplish your project goals. It is advisable to have an initial meeting with key management to review the scope of the consultant's work and affirm the goals. Management's commitment to the security project should be emphasized during this meeting. A timeline for progress reports may be discussed. It is effective to arrange for a discussion with the consultant prior to the issuance of his final written report. Management may desire that the consultant's recommendations are clearly prioritized relative to degree of importance and that the recommendations may be implemented in phases.

Some of the by-products of the work of a reputable, reliable, and knowledgeable security consultant may be:

➤ A more manageable and efficient security function
➤ Improved security accountability
➤ Coordinated and integrated security procedures, measures and controls
➤ Enhanced security awareness by tenants, employees, staff, and customers
➤ Cost-effective security measures
➤ A higher level of emergency preparedness
➤ Greater customer confidence and increased sales

To be sure, consultants are not the answer to all security problems; however, if you find a need for a security consultant, that need should be important enough for you to insure that you take the necessary steps to select a qualified professional to assist you.

Appendix A
Safety and Security Tips
for Customers

Reality is that women shoppers are more likely to become crime victims than are men. Because women are more likely than men to be mentally preoccupied with other tasks or responsibilities or may be accompanied by small children when they are shopping, and because they are *perceived* as being the weaker sex (though not necessarily always true), women are more likely to become targets or victims of criminal assailants. With this in mind, and understanding that tenants of large retail properties direct much of their advertising toward the female shopper, we are providing the following safety and security tips primarily for women:

1. Make a conscious effort to remain alert to where you are and what is going on about you AT ALL TIMES.
2. Avoid sitting in your parked car, particularly alone, for extended periods of time as you review lists or notes, read a book or talk on your cell phone.
3. Make a mental note of EXACTLY where you have parked. Use a pole marker or other reference point.
4. Try to park near a busy mall or store entrance.
5. Park in a well-lit area, preferably beneath a light fixture.
6. If you are shopping alone, wait for another shopper as you exit the mall or store and create the appearance of being together.
7. Walk with a purpose. Remain erect and alert. Avoid the appearance of being disoriented or lost.
8. Never spend an extended period of time walking about a parking lot or garage looking for a lost vehicle. Return to the store or center and seek assistance.
9. Avoid carrying multiple packages that require both hands to be occupied.
10. Don't walk alone to or from a remote parking location.
11. If available, use security escorts if you find the need.
12. Have your car key(s) in your hand as you approach your vehicle. If your vehicle

is equipped with a remote panic alarm, be prepared to use it as you walk to or from your car.

13. As you approach your vehicle, look in and about the car. Remotely turn on the interior light if possible.

14. If parked next to a van or large truck, consider entering your vehicle from the passenger side.

15. If you observe male occupant(s) sitting in a vehicle next to yours, you may consider returning to the mall or store for security assistance prior to approaching your car.

16. Avoid using remote stairwells or alleys as shortcuts.

17. Consider attaching a whistle to your key ring. If confronted by an attacker, blow the whistle loud and strong.

18. If a predator attempts to snatch your shoulder purse, let him have it. Observe him closely, get a good description and the direction of escape, and call for help. Avoid a physical confrontation and avoid injury.

19. Don't carry or display large sums of cash.

20. In a parking lot or garage, be wary of persons, particularly males, asking for directions or time of day.

21. Always lock your car doors while operating the car or while it is parked.

22. Lock packages in the trunk or out of view.

23. Keep minor children within arm's reach as you move about the center or in a store.

24. Don't let children play on escalators.

25. If confronted by a predator, consider using a physiological diversion such as: Point away and scream "Fire!" Or—Strike him with an elbow or knee to a vulnerable part of his body as you shout "No!"

While there can be no guarantee that the application of any or all of these techniques or tips will prevent a criminal act, the increased awareness that they bring may be helpful to customers, employees, tenants, vendors and visitors. Property management may want to consider developing a pamphlet with some or all of the listed safety and security tips for distribution to staff, patrons and tenants.

Appendix B
Sample Security Forms

Contained in this appendix is a sampling of some security function reports that may be used to assist in the management of a shopping center, plaza, community center or open retail environment. The sample forms may be modified to suit your specific purpose or property. While this list provides records associated with many security functions, it is not all-inclusive of every possible security task.

1. Simplified Daily Report—Motorized Security
2. Officer's Daily Log
3. Daily Security Log
4. Consolidated Monthly Security Report
5. Injury Investigation Follow-up Report
6. Release Form
7. Supervisor's Accident Investigation Report
8. Security Department Daily Report
9. Maintenance Checklist
10. Suspension Form
11. Fire Inspection Checklist
12. Motor Vehicle Accident Report
13. Missing Vehicle Report
14. Parking Violation Notices
15. Lost and Found Report
16. Towing Report
17. Customer Complaint Report
18. Tenant's Security Questionnaire
19. Staff Training Summary
20. Incident Report

1. Daily reports document such information as time on and off duty and general remarks concerning the day's activities.

Simplified Daily Report--Motorized Security

Date _____ Route _____ Vehicle no. _____

On duty _____ Mileage-start _____

Lunch hour began _____ Mileage-finish _____

Lunch hour ended _____ Gas _____ Oil _____

Off duty _____ Condition of vehicle/equipment _____

Summary of activities

Time	Activity	Location

Submitted by _____ Reviewed by _____

2.

This more detailed daily report codes various activities to coincide with similar codes shown on the Consolidated Monthly Security Report shown on Form 4.

Officer's Daily Log

Officer's Name_____ Shift # _____ Date_____ Day_____

Assignment_____ Start_____ End_____ RT_____ OT_____

Car No._____ Starting Mileage_____

Condition of Vehicle_____ Gals._____ Meter_____

Summary of Activities

Code	Activity	Total	Code	Activity	Total	Code	Activity	Total
A-1	Vehicle Missing		C-1	Investigation Conducted		D-6	Other	
A-2	Vehicle Found		C-2	Apprehensions		E-1	Bank Detail	
A-3	Vehicle Reported Stolen		C-3	Assistance Rendered		E-2	Miscellaneous Detail	
A-4	Vehicle Recovered By PD		C-4	Traffic Tickets-Customers		E-3	Apprehended Susp. Pers.	
A-5	Thefts From Vehicle		C-5	Traffic Tickets-Employees		E-4	Crime Investigation	
A-6	Vandalism To Vehicle		D-1	Cars Started		E-5	Area Inspection	
B-1	No. Of Accidents		D-2	Cars Unlocked		E-6	Fires	
B-2	No. Of Vehicles Involved		D-3	Lost Property Found		E-7	Burglar Alarms	
B-3	No. Of Pedestrians		D-4	Lost Children				
B-4	No. Of Persons Injured		D-5	First Aid				

Time	Code	Description of Every Activity Report Totaled Above

3.

This form is for on-site security to complete and fax to the off-site property manager's office.

Daily Security Log

Date _____ Days of the week _____

Emergency personnel on site: (be brief; follow-up with a detailed incident report.)

	Incident #1	Time	Incident #2	Time
Police	_____	_____	_____	_____
Fire	_____	_____	_____	_____
Paramedics	_____	_____	_____	_____

Weather conditions: First shift _____ Second shift _____

Tenant issues:
1. _____
2. _____
3. _____

Safety hazards noted:
1. _____
2. _____
3. _____

Warning stickers issued: (number)

First shift: _____ Fire lane _____ Fire lane
_____ Handicapped parking _____ Handicapped parking
_____ Other _____ Other

Lighting survey: (specify areas where lights are out)

Parking lot lights _____
Building emergency lights _____
Tenant signage _____

Contractors on site:
1. _____
2. _____
3. _____

First shift _____
Signature

Second shift _____ _____
Signature Signature

This form is to be faxed to _____
at _____ for previous day's activities.

4.

This detailed report of monthly security activities covers a wide range of security services performed. It is a vital tool for management in appraising the security operation. Totals for each activity can be obtained monthly by consulting the Officer's Daily Log, which carries the same codes. In some centers, consolidated monthly reports are distributed to all tenants.

Consolidated Monthly Security Report

Date: _____

For the Month Ending _____

Date

Personnel Report

Name	Rank	Shield No.	Assignment	Remarks

Activity Report

Security Services	This Year	Last Year
A. Vehicles		
(1) Number Reported Missing		
(2) Number Found In Parking Lots		
(3) Number Actually Stolen From Parking Lots		
(4) Number Stolen Vehicles Recovered By Police Department		
(5) Thefts From Vehicles		
(6) Vandalism to Vehicles		
B. Vehicular Accidents		
(1) Number of Vehicular Accidents		
(2) Number of Vehicles Involved		
(3) Number of Pedestrians Involved		
(4) Number of Personal Injuries		
C. Enforcement		
(1) Investigations Conducted		
(2) Apprehensions Made		
(3) Assist. Rendered to Police and/or Tenants' Sec. Depts.		
(4) Traffic Tickets Issued - Customers		
(5) Traffic Tickets Issued - Employees		

(continued)

Activity Report (cont.)

Security Services	This Year	Last Year
D. Assistance to Customers		
(1) Stalled Cars Started		
(2) Locked Cars Unlocked		
(3) Lost Property Recovered		
(4) Lost Children Found		
(5) First Aid Given		
(6) Other		
E. Assistance to Stores/Center		
(1) Bank Details		
(2) Miscellaneous Details		
(3) Apprehend Suspicious Persons		
(4) Crime Investigated		
(5) Disturbance Investigated		
(6) Area Inspection		
(7) Fires Extinguished		
(8) Burglar Alarms Answered		

Comments

Submitted By _____   Approved By _____
                    Chief of Security   Center Manager

5. This form should be used to document in detail conditions present at time of incident.

Injury Investigative Follow-up Report

Reference report # _____ Date _____ Time _____ AM/PM

Injured party's name _____

Date of injury _____ Time of injury _____ AM/PM

Exact location of injury _____

Did a security officer witness injury? ☐ Yes ☐ No

If not, who reported injury to officer? _____

Address _____

Age _____ Phone _____ Relationship _____

Injury Scene

Was scene inspected immediately following the injury? ☐ Yes ☐ No

Date of inspection _____ Time of inspection _____ AM/PM

No. of photos taken of scene _____ Officer taking photos _____

Lighting conditions (indoors/adequate lighting, indoors/poor lighting or lights not working properly, outside/daylight, outside-dusk/adequate lighting, outside-night/inadequate lighting, outside-night/bright moonlight, etc.)

_____

_____

Injury scene surface _____

Defects or obstructions in surface? ☐ Yes ☐ No Describe _____

_____

Weather conditions: Clear _____ Rain _____ Snow _____ Icy _____ Fog _____ Temp. _____

Security officer _____ Center manager _____

6. This form should be attached to form 5 (Injury Investigative Follow-up Report) if the incident results in bodily injury and the injured refuses medical assistance.

Release Form

Date _____

The security officer named below has offered to call an ambulance for me. I do not desire to go to a hospital and do not

want an ambulance. I will report to a doctor at my convenience. I understand that _____

(name of shopping center) assumes no liability for my failure to seek medical aid.

Witness _____   Individual _____

Security officer _____

7.   This form is for supervisors to fill out in the event of an accident on the premises resulting in injury to an employee.

Supervisor's Accident Investigation Report

I. General Information

Department _____   Shift _____

Employee name _____   Job title _____

Emloyee number _____   Sex (M/F) _____

Date of accident _____   Time of accident _____ AM/PM

Type of accident/illness _____

Type of injury _____   Part of body injured _____

Treatment ☐ First aid   ☐ Medical   Did employee return to work the same day? ☐ Yes ☐ No

II. Description

Where and how did accident happen? (Use additional sheets if necessary.) _____

_____

_____

_____

_____

III. Causes

Specify machine, tool, substance or object connected with the accident. _____

_____

_____

Unsafe mechanical/physical/environment condition at time of accident. (Be specific) _____

_____

_____

Personal factors (attitude, lack of knowledge or skill, slow reaction, fatigue). _____

_____

Personal protective equipment required. _____

_____

Was injured employee using required equipment? _____

_____

IV. Recommendations

Action plan to prevent recurrence (modification of machine, mechanical guarding, environment, training). _____

_____

Supervisor's signature _____   Date _____

V. Follow-up

Actions taken on recommendations (inlcude date completed). _____

_____

8. Still another type of daily report form covers only the key points in which security is involved—based upon the particular security shift. Unusual security situations are then written up in detail on other forms and iincluded as part of the daily report file.

Security Department Daily Report

Day & Date _____

Midnight to 8A.M.	Officer: _____			
Weather:	1A.M.	Clear_____	Cloudy_____	Rain/Snow_____
	3A.M.	Clear_____	Cloudy_____	Rain/Snow_____
	5A.M.	Clear_____	Cloudy_____	Rain/Snow_____

All Inside Doors OK: _____ If not, which one: _____
Locked By: _____
All Outside Doors OK: _____ If not, which one: _____
Locked By: _____
All Hatches O.K.: _____ If not, which one: _____
Make All Clock Punches _____ If not, which one: _____
Opened Mall At: _____ A.M.
Patrolled Mall and Parking Area All Night _____
Comments: _____
_____
_____

8A.M. to 4P.M.	Officer	_____		
	8A.M.	Clear_____	Cloudy_____	Rain/Snow_____
	11A.M.	Clear_____	Cloudy_____	Rain/Snow_____
	3P.M.	Clear_____	Cloudy_____	Rain/Snow_____

Patrolled Mall and Parking Area All Day _____
Comments: _____
_____
_____

4P.M. to Midnight	Officer	_____		
	5A.M.	Clear_____	Cloudy_____	Rain/Snow_____
	8P.M.	Clear_____	Cloudy_____	Rain/Snow_____
	11P.M.	Clear_____	Cloudy_____	Rain/Snow_____

All Inside Doors OK: _____ If not, which one: _____
Locked By: _____
All Outside Doors OK: _____ If not, which one: _____
Locked By: _____
Patrolled Mall and Parking Area _____
Comments: _____
_____

Turned Off Mall Lights At _____ P.M.
Made All Clock Rounds _____ If not, which one: _____
All Hatches O.K. _____ If not, which one: _____

Security Officer Signature _____
Supervisor Signature _____

9. This checklist is used to call the maintenance department's attention to a wide variety of physical problems in the center itself as well as in the common areas. Problems requiring immediate attention would be communicated to maintenance in a less formal manner.

Maintenance Checklist

To: Superintendent Of Maintenance
From: Securty Department
Subject: Traffic Safety, Miscellaneous Condition

At the location(s) indicated, the condition(s) indicated by "X" exist(s). It is recommended that appropriate action be taken to remedy such condition(s).

Location: _____

☐ Stop Signs   ☐ Broken   ☐ Defaced   ☐ Need Painting
☐ Speed Limit Signs   ☐ Broken   ☐ Defaced   ☐ Need Painting
☐ One Way Street Signs ☐ Broken   ☐ Defaced   ☐ Need Painting
☐ Parking Signs   ☐ Broken   ☐ Defaced   ☐ Need Painting
☐ Directional Arrows and/or Markers Need Repainting
☐ Crosswalks Need Repainting
☐ Stop Signs Needed Due To   ☐ Blind Corner   ☐ Heavy One-Way Traffic
☐ Crosswalk Needed Due To Heavy Pedestrian Traffic
☐ Traffic Lights   ☐ Defective   ☐ Out Of Order
☐ Curb Markings Need Repainti
☐ Restricted Parking Signs Needed
☐ Tree Branches Obstructing Signs, Hazardous Conditions
☐ Plumbing Fixtures, Facets, Leakage, etc.
☐ Lights - Parking Area - Corridor, Concourse
☐ Lights - Tenants' Signs
☐ Rubbish Accumulated
☐ Dust Accumulated
☐ Restrooms (Vandalism)
☐ Escalator Conditions
☐ Condition of Vehicles, Scooters, Trucks, Hi-Lift
☐ Other Problems (Explain in Detail)   _____

Remarks (Show Location and Action Taken or Recommended)   _____

Signed_____

Date_____ Time_____

10. Use this form only after checking its legality in your locality.

Suspension Form

Date: _____

I, _____ , _____ of
                                    (name)   (age/DOB)

_____   _____
                            (address)   (phone)

do hereby acknowledge that I am not permitted upon the property of ABC Shopping Center. I am aware that if I am found on the property before the suspension has expired, I will be subject to arrest for criminal trespass. I also acknowledge that I am not permitted on the property for a period of:

_____ from _____ (date)   to _____ (date)
      days, month(s) or year(s)

for the following reason: _____
                                                              (offense)

This notice will be filed with center security. I agree by my signature hereon to save free and harmless and hold blameless ABC Shopping Center and owner lessors of said shopping center from and against any and all claims, demands, or actions or damage resulting from this incident.

_____
                            (signature of individual)

_____
          (signature of parent or guardian, if under 18 years of age

_____
                            (witness)

_____
                            (witness)

Police Report # _____

11. Each tenant's space should be inspected quarterly to make sure tenants are reminded to be safety conscious. A copy of this report should be sent to tenant's corporate offices.

Fire Inspection Checklist

I. General information

Name of facility _____   Date _____

Name of store _____   Manager's name _____

Inspector's name _____   Inspection date _____

II. Additional information

Are additional sprinklers present? ☐ Yes ☐ No   Are sprinklers clear of dust and obstructions? ☐ Yes ☐ No

Comments _____
_____
_____
_____
_____

Are chemicals/paint/hazardous materials stored on site in the proper containers?   ☐ Yes ☐ No

Comments _____
_____
_____
_____
_____

Are fire safety markings on all appropriate doors?   ☐ Yes ☐ No

Comments _____
_____
_____
_____
_____

Are there sufficient fire extinguishers in the area?   ☐ Yes ☐ No

What type are they? _____
_____
_____

Have fire extinguishers been inspected regularly?   ☐ Yes ☐ No

Comments _____
_____
_____
_____

(continued)

Are there smoke detectors in the closed-up storage areas/areas where chemicals, etc. are stored? ☐ Yes ☐ No

Comments _____

_____

_____

_____

_____

_____

_____

Additional information _____

_____

_____

_____

_____

_____

_____

_____

Inspector _____ Date _____

Inspector _____ Date _____

Store manager/employee _____ Date _____

12. Information about motor vehicle accidents is often recorded separately from other types of accidents.

Motor Vehicle Accident Report

Information Exchange For Accidents On Private Property

Date of Accident: Month _____ Day _____ Year _____ Day of Week _____
Time: _____ Place Where Accident Occurred: _____
Road Conditions: _____ Reporting Security Officer _____

It is important that diagram be completed. Show street names, direction, vehicles, buildings, etc.
Draw your own diagram if necessary.

X=Point of Impact   T = Traffic Light   S = Stop Sign   Y=Yield Sign   35=Speed Limit   ➤ Indicate North by Arrow

Accident Information

Vehicle #1 Driver Name _____ Phone _____
Address _____
City, State, Zip _____
Insurance Co. _____ Agent _____
Address of Insurance Co. _____ Phone _____
Vehicle Make _____ Model/Year _____ Color _____ License No. _____ State _____
Vehicle Identification Number _____ Driver's License No. _____
State _____ Damage - Circle F - R

Vehicle #2 Driver Name _____ Phone _____
Address _____
City, State, Zip _____
Insurance Co. _____ Agent _____
Address of Insurance Co. _____ Phone _____
Vehicle Make _____ Model/Year _____ Color _____ License No. _____ State _____
Vehicle Identification Number _____ Driver's License No. _____
State _____ Damage - Circle F - R

Police Notified ☐ Yes ☐ No Officer Name _____ Badge No. _____
First Aid Squad at Scene ☐ Yes ☐ No
Additional Information - Injured, Property Damage, etc. _____
_____

Citation Issued _____

Use Reverse side if necessary   Signature of Reporting Officer _____

13. This form records information about customers' cars that are reported missing while parked at the center. It is intended primarily for internal use. Most centers will assist customers by touring the parking areas to determine if the car has been stolen and then putting the customer in touch with local police.

Missing Vehicle Report

Date of Report _____

Vehicle Make _____   Year of Car _____

Vehicle Identification No. _____   Motor No. _____

License No. _____ Year _____   State _____

Color _____   Body Style _____

Owner _____   Address _____

Home Phone _____   Work Phone _____

Missing From _____   Date Reported Missing _____

Estimated Value of Car _____

Identifiable Objects in Car _____

_____

_____

Report Given To _____

_____

Remarks: _____

_____

_____

_____

_____

_____

_____

_____

_____

Reported to Police Department: ☐ YES ☐ NO

Officer's Name: _____   Signed _____

Badge Number: _____   (Security Officer)

Report Number: _____

Approved by _____

(Chief of Security)

14. This page shows two types of forms used for parking violations. The form on the left warns of parking violations within the center. In cases of serious violations the car may be towed away. The form is perforated so that the stub on the right can be retained to keep a record of repeat offenders. The form on the right is a notice that is placed on car windshields. The backing of it, which is removed before application, can be imprinted with basic information to retain (date, time, location, plate number, model, etc.).

Parking Violation Notices

Vehicle _____ License _____
Date _____ Time _____

WARNING

You have violated Traffic Regulations as indicated:
1. Improperly Parked in Stall ☐
2. Parked in Roadway ☐
3. Parked in Handicapped Zone ☐
4. Blocking Traffic ☐
5. Parked in Truck Dock ☐
6. Employee in Customer Area ☐

In the interest of safety and convenience your cooperation is invited in observing regulations on reverse side.

Front

Violation No. _____
Type _____
Time _____
Date _____
Location _____
License Tag # _____
Make _____
Color _____
Officer _____

The Center has been planned for shopping ease. To provide safe and convenient parking all the following regulations must be observed.

Traffic Regulations
Obey Stop and Yield Signs
Obey Directional Arrows
Obey Speed Signs

Parking Regulations
Park Cars Nose-in to Center of Stall
No Parking Along Curbs
No Parking in Painted Crosshatch Markings

Safety Regulations
Drive Carefully - Be Alert
Hand Brake on Tightly When Parked
Observe Courtesy of the Road   *Back*

THIS VEHICLE IS IMPROPERLY PARKED

CENTER REGULATIONS STATE THAT IMPROPERLY PARKED VEHICLES MAY BE SUBJECT TO BEING TOWED AWAY AT THE OWNER'S EXPENSE. THIS VEHICLE IS IMPROPERLY PARKED:

☐ BLOCKING FIRE LANE   ☐ IN LOADING ZONE
☐ BLOCKING BUILDING ENTRANCE   ☐ IN THE HANDICAPPED ZONE
☐ OTHER _____

YOUR LICENSE TAG NUMBER HAS BEEN RECORDED AND REPEATED VIOLATIONS WILL CAUSE YOUR VEHICLE TO BE REMOVED.

15. This dual form not only serves to record pertinent information on the item lost (including name of person reporting the loss or find) but also makes provision for recording details on its eventual disposition. Some centers use a separate receipt form when releasing an article.

Lost and Found Report

Report no. _____ Recovered _____

Tiime _____ AM/PM   Location _____ Date _____

Individuals accepting and handling property: Security officer _____
(name)

Store employee _____
(store)

Property is   ☐ Lost   ☐ Found
Notified by: Name _____
Address _____
City, State, ZIP _____   Home phone _____   Work phone _____

☐ Check here if above does not care to be known.   Owner of property?   ☐ Yes   ☐ No

Description of property _____

Disposition of property after 60 days _____

Form To Be Filled Out by Person Claiming Lost Property

(in receipt)
I hereby certify that I am   (the legal owner)   of the above property _____
(the legal agent of the owner)

☐ Check here if property is intact.

List any property not received _____

Name _____   Date _____
Address _____   Time _____
City, State, ZIP _____   Home Phone _____   Work phone _____

Employee or officer giving release sign here _____ Date _____

Person claiming lost property sign here _____ Date _____

16.

If vehicle towing is authorized by management, use this form to detail pertinent facts.

Towing Report

I. General Information

Who requested tow? _____

Trade name of retailer requesting tow _____

Security officer's name _____

License number _____

V.I.N. number _____

Make of vehicle _____

Date of tow _____ Time of tow _____ AM/PM

II. Description

Why is vehicle being towed? _____

Management person(s) authorizing tow? _____

Who has been called to tow vehicle? _____

Where was vehicle towed? _____

Please list other pertinent facts _____

Security officer's signature _____ Date _____

17. Property managers should be made aware of customers' complaints in order to avoid future complaints and foster good customer relations by following up with complainant.

Customer Complaint Report

I. General Information

Type of complaint: ☐ Security ☐ Operations ☐ Marketing ☐ Merchant

Date _____

Customer name _____

Address _____

_____

Telephone number _____

II. Description

Detailed complaint _____

_____

_____

_____

_____

III. Recommendations

Action plan to prevent recurrence _____

_____

_____

_____

_____

IV. Follow-Up

Action taken on recommendation _____

_____

_____

_____

_____

Preparer's signature _____ Date _____

Complainant's signature _____ Date _____

18.

Detailed information on each store's internal security measures should be maintained by center management and made available to center security officers. This form records the significant information.

Tenant's Security Questionnaire

Date _____

Name of Tenant _____

Address _____ Phone _____

Is Tenant Division or Subsidiary of Larger Corporation? ☐ Yes ☐ No

Name of Corporation _____

Address of Corporate Offices _____

Principal Business _____

Name of Store Owner or Store Manager _____ Home Phone _____

Assistant _____ Home Phone _____

Approximate Number of Employees _____

Does Tenant Have Burglar and Fire Alarm Protection? ☐ Yes ☐ No

Name of Burglar Alarm Company _____ Phone _____

Name of Fire Alarm Company _____ Phone _____

Burglar Alarms Ring at: ☐ Police Headquarters ☐ Central Station ☐ Outside Bell

Fire Alarms Ring at: ☐ Fire or Police Station ☐ Central Station ☐ Outside Bell

Does Tenant Have Own Security Department? ☐ Yes ☐ No Agency _____

Name of Security Manager _____ Home Phone _____

Assistant _____ Home Phone _____

In case of Emergency, Shopping Center Security/Management Should Contact the Following Personnel:

1. _____ Home Phone _____

2. _____ Home Phone _____

3. _____ Home Phone _____

4. _____ Home Phone _____

19.

This form helps track the hours spent on staff training and the subjects covered, thereby helping to pinpoint areas that require more review.

Staff Training Summary

Summary for (name) _____

Subject	Date	Total Hours	Training Officer	Comments
Security Manual and Patrolling				
Security Meeting Auto theft report; suggest ways to combat; roof procedures; lost and found; daily activity reports; vehicle and incident reports. Law: felony vs. misdemeanor; propety ownership; theft				
Security Meeting Report writing; auto theft; feedback				
Security Meeting Uniforms; schedules; reports; distribution; operations; vehicles; cleanliness; time cards				
Security Meeting Manual: legal section; report writing; accidents; opening and closing reports; patrol patterns; restrooms; roof procedure				
Security Meeting Radio log; procedures; patrol patterns to combat auto theft; roof entry procedures; parking violations; fire panel				
Security Meeting Security manual; review of daily procedures				
Security Meeting Report writing; incidents; traffic accidents; review legal section				
Security Meeting Daily activity reports; traffic and parking rules; ticket writing; radio procedure; patrol patterns; handling children; merchandise transfer				
Security Meeting Patrol patterns; foot and vehicle responding to wreckers; roof procedure; giving descriptions; maintaining equipment				
Security Meeting Daily activity logs; vehicle patrol patterns; new concepts; foot patrol patterns; radio procedure; handling equipment, e.g., trucks, radios; personnel				
Security Meeting Report writing; incidents' review; understanding criminal trespass; feedback				
CPR (Cardiopulmonary Resuscitation)				
Security Meeting Security manual; review security policy and daily procedures				

Signature _____ Date _____

License no. _____ State _____ Expiration date _____

20.

Incident Report

Incident file Number: (year and sequential number ex. 20-001) _____

Reporting Officer: _____ Date: _____ Time: _____

Date of Occurrence: _____

Time of Occurence: _____   Weather Conditions: clear, bright sun, cloudy, rain, snow, fog, strong winds, freezing

Day of Week: _____   (CIRCLE ONE)

Incident Category

Alteration	_____	Medical Assist	_____	Slip/Fall	_____
Auto Theft	_____	Missing Person	_____	Fire	_____
Auto Accident	_____	Fight	_____	Police Assist	_____
Fraud/Forgery	_____	Faulty/Inoperable	_____		
		Trespass	_____		
Theft	_____	Alarm Response	_____	Vandalism	_____
Guest Complaint Other_____					

Incident Location
(zone & specific location)

_____

_____

_____

Complainant/Victim/Injured Party

Name (last, First, MI) _____

Street Address _____

City, State, Zip _____

Home Phone _____ **Work Phone** _____

Date of Birth _____ **Sex M or F**

Social Security Number _____

Witness

Name (last, First, MI) _____

Street Address _____

City, State, Zip _____

Home Phone _____ **Work Phone** _____

Date of Birth _____ **Sex M or F**

Social Security Number _____

(continued)

Additional Witnesses

Name (last, First, MI) _____

Street Address _____

City, State, Zip _____

Home Phone _____ Work Phone _____

Date of Birth _____ Sex M or F

Social Security Number _____

Narrative of Incident [details—who, what, when, where]

_____

_____

_____

_____

_____

_____

_____

_____

_____

_____

_____

_____

_____

_____

_____

_____

Bibliography

The following publications provide excellent foundation material that may be used to enhance your security management skills, and thus your entire security function.

Published by Butterworth Heinmann
Available through the American Society for Industrial Security
➢ *Crime Prevention Through Environmental Design*—by Timothy Crowe
➢ *Effective Security Management, 4th Edition*—by Charles A. Sennewald
➢ *The Effective Security Supervision Manual, 2nd Edition*—by Ralph Brislin
➢ *Guard Force Management*—by Lucien G. Canton
➢ *150 Things You Should Know About Security*—by Louis A. Tyska and Lawrence J. Fennelly
➢ *Outsourcing Security*—by John D. Stees
➢ *Risk Analysis and the Security Survey, 2nd Edition*—by James F. Broder
➢ *Security and Crime Prevention*—by Robert L. O'Block
➢ *Security Operations Management*—by Robert D. McCrie
➢ *Understanding Crime Prevention*—by National Crime Prevention Institute

Published by and available through the American Society for Industrial Security
➢ *Emergency Planning Handbook, 2nd Edition*—by ASIS Disaster Management Council

Published by the American Bar Association
➢ *A Complete Guide to Premises Security Litigation, 2nd Edition*—Alan Kaminsky